P9-CQL-122

BE A LEADER PEOPLE FOLLOW

David L. Hocking

A Division of GL Publications
Ventura, CA U.S.A.

Other good reading:
>*Your Spiritual Gifts Can Help Your Church Grow*
>   by C. Peter Wagner
>*Your Church Can Grow* by C. Peter Wagner
>*The Measure of a Church* by Gene A. Getz
>*Your Church Has Real Possibilities*
>   by Robert H. Schuller
>*How to Grow a Church*
>   by Donald A. MacGavran and Win C. Arn
>*Love, Acceptance and Forgiveness*
>   by Jerry Cook with Stanley C. Baldwin

The foreign language publishing of all Regal books is under the direction of Gospel Literature International GLINT. GLINT provides financial and technical help for the adaptation, translation and publishing of books for millions of people worldwide. For information regarding translation, contact: GLINT, P.O. Box 6688, Ventura, California 93006.

Scripture quotations are from the *New American Standard Bible*. © The Lockman Foundation 1960, 1962, 1963, 1968, 1971, 1972, 1973, 1975. Used by permission.

Fourth Printing, 1983

Published by Regal Books
A Division of GL Publications
Ventura, California 93006
Printed in U.S.A.

Library of Congress Catalog Card No. 78-67854
ISBN 0-8307-0680-1

To the members of Grace Brethren Church in Long Beach, California, believers who have known me from my birth into this world and have watched me grow to the point of serving them as their pastor, patiently enduring my struggles with spiritual leadership, I affectionately dedicate this book.

To those scores of faithful staff members with whom I have served these many years and who know my weaknesses as a spiritual leader, yet have supported and loved me in spite of it all, I dedicate this book.

To the students who sat under my teaching of leadership and often wondered if I knew what I was talking about, I dedicate this book.

To spiritual leaders everywhere who, like me, desire to be more effective in their leadership of God's people and understand their need of help, I dedicate this book.

CONTENTS

PREFACE

It was in the third grade in a military academy where I learned to swim. The instructor made me jump in the pool at the deep end. It is amazing how quickly one can learn to adjust to the problems of life! I have never forgotten that lesson. The instructor knew more about me than I thought at that time. He knew that with me it was "sink or swim." Leadership is like that—some of us have to learn the hard way!

Like most people, I have been exposed to various leadership responsibilities (some of which I would like to forget!). Through them all, I have often wondered what makes a good leader. From the joys and heartaches of starting a church and watching it grow to my present responsibilities as senior pastor of a large church and school system with some 150 employees and a budget in excess of two million dollars per year, I still wonder what it takes to make a good leader! Even though I have taught leadership to graduate school students, I still wonder.

Without God's help, none of us could ever hope to be what God describes as a spiritual leader. It seems like two out of every three decisions I make don't turn out the way I thought. However, I have learned some valuable principles which I have put down on paper. Maybe you need to do the same. Some things are essentials in this matter of leadership, and other things you can take or leave. It is my prayer that you will study the essentials I have listed in this book in the light of what God's Word teaches and your own experience verifies. Perhaps you will agree that these things are necessary and will make us all better leaders.

David L. Hocking
1979

PART I

EXAMPLE:
CAN PEOPLE
DEPEND ON YOUR
LEADERSHIP?

WHAT KIND OF AN EXAMPLE SHOULD A SPIRITUAL LEADER BE?

My first idea of a leader was my dad. He was strong and believed in discipline. He loved people and often helped them in time of need. He was not well-educated, but he seemed to understand people. He was committed to the Lord's work and gave freely of his money to support it. I remember his hands. They were rough from the hours of hard labor he experienced in the oil fields. His hands were always doing things, and sometimes it seemed to me as a boy that my dad's character was in those hands. They still remind me of who he was and what he did. He now is with the Lord.

Next came my pastor. He was soft-spoken, loving and kind. He always seemed to have time for people. When he preached, he seemed to be talking with you as though you were the only one in the auditorium. He constantly encouraged me and followed my growth in the Lord. When I was away in college, he wrote me letters. I had the joy of working with him on his staff and observing him up close. He was special and still is. I am now serving as his pastor—what an honor!

There were many others along the way who manifested leadership to me, but the day came when I needed answers to some questions: What is a spiritual leader? How do you know one when you see one? What was God's idea of a leader? So I had to turn to the Bible for answers and I started with the Old Testament.

Old Testament Examples of Leadership

Moses was the first to capture my attention. In Exodus 18 he received some good advice from his father-in-law, Jethro, who was a priest of Midian. Jethro told him that he was wearing himself out by trying to handle everything himself. The people were also weary of this method. Whenever you see a situation like this, where one person is trying to do it all himself, there is a need for leadership.

One of the fallacies of human nature is that we do not see ourselves as others see us. We do not like to admit there is something we cannot do. If the situation, like that of Moses, does not change and responsibilities are not shared with others, then the "Peter Principle" sets in very quickly. That principle of modern business deals with people rising to their level of incompetence! The tragedy is that many people cannot face this fact, and as a result, they become the major obstacle to further growth or progress.

I can identify easily with Moses. I would rather do it myself than have others do it. But that doesn't mean that I do it better! In fact, I have often suffered because I did not allow others to help. When it comes down to the bottom line, it's usually an ego problem. I don't want to admit that I can't handle a situation, or I want others to see how capable I really am!

The first thing Moses had to do was to clarify his own job description. Job descriptions should always begin at the top and work down through other levels in the organization. They should be simple, clear, and flexible. According to Exodus 18:19-21, Moses had three major responsibilities: (1) to bring the problems of the people to God; (2) to teach them the way they should walk and train them in the work they are to do; (3) to select able leaders to help him bear the burden of leadership.

Sound simple? That's the way it should be! Too often the main leader becomes wrapped up in details that other workers should handle, thus diminishing the effectiveness of his own life and responsibilities. Sometimes, as in the case of Moses, it is hard to let go of things you are doing until someone in whom you have confidence explains to you the danger of trying to do it all yourself.

At one point in my ministry I was following the "Moses syndrome." I was not delegating to others and, frankly, I was exhausted by the many things I was doing. A trusted friend and co-worker came to me one day and said, "David, what will we ever do when you die?" That did it. It was hard to admit, but I was the problem. Too much depended upon me, and I was not indispensable. We made some immediate changes that resulted in continued growth.

Moses also had to know what qualities to look for in leaders who could help him (see Exod. 18:21). He had to look for (1) men who feared God, (2) men of truth, and (3) men who hated dishonest gain.

There is no reference in these qualifications to educational background or any particular skills or talents. These qualities represent men who can be trusted and followed. It is a godly life-style that counts!

After Moses died, the Lord spoke to Joshua and told him that he would lead His people to the land which He was giving them. Deuteronomy 34:9 says that Joshua had been chosen by Moses to take his place.

Joshua was "filled with the spirit of wisdom." In Joshua 1 there is a list of qualifications he would need

12

for effective leadership: (1) spiritual strength and courage (see Josh. 1:6,7,9); (2) constant meditation in God's Word (see Josh. 1:8); and (3) uncompromising obedience to God's commands (see Josh. 1:7,8). God said that if these qualities are in Joshua's life, he can expect prosperity and success.

Too many Christian leaders today are trying to operate in their own strength and are compromising on the plain teaching of the Word of God. Joshua was told, "Do not turn from it to the right or to the left." Any slight departure or deviation from God's Word will result in a loss of leadership at that point.

Many years ago I had a friend in the ministry who began to deviate from God's Word in a certain area. We talked about it and even prayed together. For a time, his leadership continued to be strong and well supported. He justified violating the Word of God on the basis of what appeared to be the blessing of God upon his ministry. God was patient with him, and gave him many opportunities to get right with Him. One thing led to another and before too long he developed a pattern of violating the Word of God. I was not surprised to learn of his departure from the ministry and the failure of his leadership in a critical situation. We must learn the lesson God revealed to Joshua. Success according to God is based upon uncompromising obedience to His Word.

God chose David because he had internal strength. When Samuel came to anoint one of Jesse's sons to be king of Israel, he took one look at Eliab and thought, "Surely the Lord's anointed is before Him" (1 Sam. 16:6). However, God responded: "Do not look at his appearance or at the height of his stature, because I have rejected him; for God sees not as man sees, for man looks at the outward appearance, but the Lord looks at the heart" (1 Sam. 16:7).

13

How true that is! In choosing a leader, we look for the attractive person. We speak of "charisma" or "great personality." We like the one who speaks eloquently and is neatly dressed. Leadership to us is often a matter of outward appearance. While these things are not sinful in themselves and certainly traits to be desired, they often become the most important factors in determining the spiritual leader. But, according to God Himself, the most important ingredient is internal, in the heart, not external.

After a 40-year reign as king of Israel, David approached death. He called his son, Solomon, to him and charged him to walk in the ways of the Lord, keep His statutes and commandments and His judgments and His testimonies. God told Solomon that he needed a godly life-style through commitment to His commandments. Then He would establish his throne and kingdom (see 2 Chron. 7:17-20). Once again the example of a spiritual leader is set before us.

We could speak of many others in Israel's history and of the lessons they learned. It is easy to say that these men of the Old Testament were "super saints" and not like you and me. But, James 5:17 reminds us of Elijah, the great prophet of God, who was a man "with a nature like ours." The men of the Old Testament had problems like you and I do. What God told them about spiritual leadership applies to us as well. We're not perfect, but neither were they. We need God's help, and so did they. What God demanded of them, He demands of us. The example of the leader is fundamental to the effectiveness of what he says and does. It is crucial to the people who must depend upon that leadership.

New Testament Examples of Leadership
In the New Testament, the concepts of leadership are

developed from the standards set forth for elders (or bishops) and deacons. In Acts 6:1-7 we learn that because of the growth ("disciples were increasing in number") of the church there were certain administrative problems demanding additional leadership help. When the apostles called the believers together to consider the problem, they challenged them to select seven men from among themselves.

The best kind of a leader is one chosen by the people he leads. He comes from their own number. They know him and have observed his life-style. Acts 6:3 says there should be a time for observing their conduct before they are selected for leadership. The words "of good reputation" refer to those who have been constantly witnessed or watched by others.

These men were to be full of the Holy Spirit, wisdom, and faith. It doesn't mean they were perfect. It means they manifested these qualities as habits of life. There should be a period of time in which the good seed of God's Word can bring forth recognizable fruit. Leaders need wisdom and faith, and that comes through experience and maturity. Without faith, there will be little growth, vision, or outreach. Without wisdom, many wrong decisions will be made. Placing new converts into leadership is not wise. Their leadership traits as believers have not had enough time to develop and become obvious to others.

As a young pastor trying to start a church, I knew we needed spiritual leaders, but I wasn't sure how to go about it. A man was chosen for leadership who was a new believer. In the world's eyes, he was qualified. He was influential, wealthy, and well-educated. In every way, he appeared to be successful. Well, I learned the hard way that spiritual leaders are made over a period of time, not born! He constantly had problems with situations and people in the church. He did not understand, and he lacked maturity in dealing with others. He did not see things from God's viewpoint but rather from the advantage of one with worldly wisdom. He has grown much in the years that followed, and we both look back to that time with greater understanding.

Paul's Advice on Leadership

Paul knew the importance of the leader's example. He said (Phil. 4:9), "The things you have learned and received and heard and seen in me, practice these things; and the God of peace shall be with you." In Hebrews 13:7 he wrote: "Remember those who led you, who spoke the word of God to you; and considering the outcome of their way of life, imitate their faith."

A classic example of Paul's advice to leaders is found in Acts 20. He called the elders of the church in Ephesus to meet with him at a place called Miletus. In that beautiful talk he continually reminded them of his own example of leadership. He wanted them to follow his steps, to do and live as he had done among them. That's the secret of good leadership— following the example of the leader.

I was reminded of this important truth one day when I stopped a little boy in the hall of our Sunday School building and said, "What do you want to be when you grow up?" Without a moment's hesitation he said, "Just like my dad!" How fortunate that dad! What an honor to have your son respond like that! That little boy was so proud of his dad, and he wanted to follow his dad's example. Again, that's what real leadership is all about!

Paul said to Timothy, "And the things which you have heard from me in the presence of many witnesses, these entrust to faithful men, who will be able to teach others also" (2 Tim. 2:2). The words "from me" are literally "alongside of me." Timothy was able to observe Paul's example and to learn about leadership through what Paul did. That's the same method our Lord used. In Mark 3:14 it says, "And He appointed twelve, that they might be with Him." Christ gave His apostles an example to follow.

What kind of example should a spiritual leader be? All these examples show one important truth. The way a leader lives speaks so loudly that you can't always hear what he says. It is a godly life-style that makes a spiritual leader what he ought to be so others can depend upon his leadership. A leader must be obedient to God's Word and follow the example of men like Moses, Joshua, David, Paul, and, of course, Jesus Christ! A leader must walk with God—be a man of prayer and be obedient to God. He must recognize that the way he lives before others is a key to his leadership. May God make us all what He wants us to be!

Leader's Checklist

1. Do you, like Moses, try to do it all by yourself?
2. Can you name someone whom you have trained to help you?
3. Is your job description like that of Moses? How is it different?
4. Are you violating a known principle of God's Word in the exercise of your leadership? In what way?
5. Is your example before others leading them to live for God? List three ways you can tell.
6. Do others have the opportunity to be with you in order to observe your example or do you remain aloof from people? List six ways you regularly open yourself up to others.
7. Do you really believe that the example of your life should be followed by others? Why?

2 HOW TO RECOGNIZE A SPIRITUAL LEADER

Several years ago my faith and confidence in a certain Christian leader was shattered. I could hardly believe that he was not the spiritual leader I had always thought him to be. This caused me to ask the question I have asked many times since: "How do you recognize a spiritual leader?" How can I be sure that a person is a spiritual leader instead of just putting on an act in front of others? Let's face it—that question has troubled all of us at one time or another.

One day it dawned on me that the qualifications of 1 Timothy 3 for elders (bishops) and deacons was the answer to recognizing spiritual leaders. These qualities are not just for the select few, but represent what a godly man is really like. These are standards for everyone, and especially for leaders. The way to select or recognize a spiritual leader is to check out his life-style with 1 Timothy 3 and see if he manifests these traits as a habit of life. Of course, no one is perfect. There will be moments of weakness and failure. But, the key is whether or not there is an overall pattern of life that reflects these qualities. A person could fool you at any one given moment of time, but it is quite difficult to deceive those who live with you and know you over a long period of time.

When a person is filled with the Spirit and obedient to the Word, these qualities will be reflected in that person's life. Each of these traits mentioned are important and worthy of detailed study. Any person who desires to be a spiritual leader should constantly refer to this listing in 1 Timothy 3 (also Titus 1) for guidance and direction.

Do You Desire to Be a Spiritual Leader?

First Timothy 3:1 tells us that there will be a continual desire for spiritual leadership. The Greek words used suggest an intense desire, reaching out after a goal. It isn't a momentary fancy, but rather something that stays with you. When God calls you to leadership, there is no lightning bolt in the sky or bells ringing. God plants a continual desire in your heart. No one needs to keep motivating you to leadership. You begin to experience self-motivation. Experience shows us that those who do not have a continual desire for leadership will usually fail in a crisis or give up when things get tough.

One of the young men in our church who had been placed in a position of leadership was failing to motivate others or to get people to respond to his leadership. He became deeply depressed and discouraged. He began to question his own leadership and doubt that God had ever called him. When we finally talked about it, the root of the problem was the lack of desire in his heart for spiritual leadership. He simply did not want it. He did not want to pay the price of leadership or face the risks involved. After some counsel, he stepped out of that role of leadership and assumed the role of following others. Happiness returned to him, and he once again had the peace of God in his life. Leadership is not for

19

everyone. The demands are great. The pressures are so intense at times that apart from knowing God has called you, you could easily throw in the towel.

Everyone has experienced at one time or another a desire to be a leader. But, real spiritual leadership must be based upon a constant desire. You want to be a leader more than anything else! God's call is deeply impressed upon your heart and you think about it all the time. That's desire!

How Long Have You Been a Christian?

It takes maturity and experience to be a spiritual leader. First Timothy 3:9 says that deacons must be "holding to the mystery of the faith with a clear conscience." A spiritual leader must be settled in his own commitment to the gospel of Christ and the doctrines of God's Word without any hesitation. A man who doubts his relationship to Christ will not be a spiritual leader to others.

One of the men in our church was struggling with a man he led to Christ. He wanted to disciple him but ran into many problems. The one he led to Christ began to grow and develop and soon was more mature than the one who was to be his spiritual leader. When the situation finally came to my attention I realized that the first man was having problems because of his own lack of security and assurance as to his relationship with Christ. It is difficult to be a spiritual leader to someone else when there is a lack of confidence in your own heart about your commitment to Christ.

First Timothy 3:6 says that one who aspires to an office of leadership should not be "a new convert, lest he become conceited and fall into the condemnation incurred by the devil." A position of leadership can easily lead to pride in the heart of the new convert.

Maturity can see things differently and with proper attitudes. First Timothy 3:10 adds, "And let these also first be tested." The testing here is for the purpose of receiving approval. People who have been under trial and testing and have proven themselves faithful under these conditions will make the best leaders every time!

An overseer (bishop) should be "above reproach," according to 1 Timothy 3:2. The Greek word refers to a specific charge against someone. The idea of this quality in one's life is that there should be no specific charge of violating God's Word that can be brought against that person. Of course, it doesn't mean he is perfect! It means that all affairs are in order with no loose ends around, like unresolved conflicts and problems from the past. Then Paul adds, "And he must have a good reputation with those outside the church, so that he may not fall into reproach and the snare of the devil" (1 Tim. 3:7). Spiritual leaders must have a consistent testimony and life-style among nonbelievers as well as believers.

One of my friends in the ministry lost his leadership because of bad debts. He got himself into such financial trouble that his testimony and reputation were destroyed in that community and his church suffered deeply in the process.

Maturity takes time. You don't become a leader in one day! Be patient while others have the chance to watch you as you grow and minister in the Body of Christ. Spiritual leadership is no place for a new believer.

Your Marriage Affects Your Leadership

What you are like in your home often reveals your right to a position of leadership. Those who know us best live with us every day. First Timothy 3:2 says that the leader must be "the husband of one wife." (See also 1

Tim. 3:12.) There are all kinds of views about that phrase including issues like polygamy, divorce, and re-marriage. Literally, the phrase reads, "a one-woman man." Devotion without question is the way I read that! There should be no doubt in people's minds about your loyalty and love for your marital partner!

My wife is my best friend. She loves me in spite of what she knows about me and our love has deepened through the many years of our marriage. We are both thankful. She doesn't realize as much as I the impor-tance of her life and love to my leadership. Something would depart out of my leadership without her loving companionship and support. She's always there. I love to go home. I don't know all the joys we will experience in heaven, but the love between my wife and me has got to be close! Having said that doesn't mean we don't have problems like everyone else; we do! But we both understand the importance of our commitment and companionship to one another as it relates to spiritual leadership.

Tragedies in marriages are always hard to accept, and especially when they happen to spiritual leaders. We all have examples that have broken our hearts. Perhaps we would do ourselves a favor if we insisted on a stronger evidence for marital fidelity in the lives of those we select for leadership rather than the simple fact that they are married or that they have never been divorced.

The leader's commitment and love for his marital partner reveals much about the kind of leadership he has with others. If strong love is not evident in the marriage, it may also be absent in the leader's relationships to those around him. If he is critical of his wife, he will probably be critical of those with whom he works and ministers to. Yes, your marriage does affect your leader-ship!

Do Your Children Respond to Your Leadership?

First Timothy 3:4,5 reveals that a man cannot really take care of the church if he can't take care of his own children. But what does that mean? Are parents responsible for the sins of their children? Ezekiel 18:20 says no. Parents are responsible to manage their children, but even under the best parental care, some children rebel (they have a sin nature too, you know) and break their parents' hearts. The quality in a leader's life that reveals his ability to lead others is seen in the way he handles his children. First Timothy 3:4 uses the word "manage," which means literally "to stand before" others. It refers to a leader who motivates and challenges others. It refers also to training and teaching. In other words, according to this text, a spiritual leader should have a father's heart, he is to keep his children under control with all dignity; he has a certain seriousness of mind and purpose about him; he is calm, purposeful, and stable—his control is not that of a tyrant who screams and yells at his children. He manages with dignity and self-control.

Every time I get angry at what my children have done I get this gnawing feeling inside that I just disqualified myself for the ministry of leadership! It usually affects me right about the time of disciplining my children. Was I too harsh? Did I spank too hard? Did I listen to their side of the story? Was I calm, cool, and collected? The devil would love to have me stop disciplining my children, but I know that discipline is necessary and reveals my love for them. But, it can also reveal my problems. Sometimes I am angry without reason other than personal inconvenience. Your children can respond to you out of fear rather than respect or love. A certain amount of godly fear is necessary, I suppose, but sometimes there is a fine line between what is good and what is bad.

Proverbs 13:24 says, "He who spares his rod hates his son, but he who loves him disciplines him diligently." But on the other side, Ephesians 6:4 says, "And, fathers, do not provoke your children to anger; but bring them up in the discipline and instruction of the Lord." How we need the wisdom of God!

It seems to me that the basic idea that a man's leadership is affected by his family life depends on how he deals with them in various situations. Does he apply discipline when it's needed? If he doesn't, then he will lack the courage or understanding in applying biblical discipline to believers who are not walking with the Lord. Does he talk with his children? Do they feel free to talk with him? This will obviously affect his communication with those under his leadership. Does he demonstrate love for his children, spending time with them, doing things together? If this is missing, the leader will probably be that way in his relationships with others. Again, taking care of your family is essential in order to take care of other believers.

How Do You Feel About Yourself?

There are two traits mentioned in 1 Timothy 3 that deal with your attitudes and reactions toward yourself and your abilities.

The first trait is that a leader should be temperate. A temperate person is sober and calm in judgment; clear in thinking and perspective. He is someone who is stable and does not overreact to situations, becoming overwhelmed, nervous, or insecure. A leader who is insecure will make others insecure. If he is nervous under pressure, everyone else will be also.

This came to my attention as an important leadership trait when I was confronted with a serious situation and said, "What are we ever going to do?" A co-worker said,

"We? You're the leader!" Suddenly I realized what temperate means. When confronted with the situation by myself I felt nervous, insecure, and wondered how in the world we could ever handle that problem. A leader must learn to be calm and to think through things from God's perspective, not man's.

A second trait is that a leader should be prudent. A prudent person has a quality of mind that is humble and sound in its evaluations of his own abilities and gifts. There are two extremes to be avoided when looking at this quality. One extreme happens when Christians see themselves as nothing. They are worthless. They forget what God sees. He knows our sin and weakness but He also sees our value and worth—that's why He redeemed us! We are valuable to Him, and we belong to Him! He wants us to glorify Him in the bodies that He purchased (see 1 Cor. 6:19,20). A prudent leader is one who knows that he has value because of what God has already done in his life, and what He can do in the future. The other extreme happens when believers have an exalted view of themselves. They ignore the grace of God and start boasting in their own abilities and talents. How sad when conceit and feelings of self-importance take over in a spiritual leader's life!

I sat in the office of a Christian leader one day, admiring the many accomplishments in his life and ministry. When I asked, "To what do you attribute your success?" he proceeded to tell me about his educational background, his talents, his way with people, his good business sense, etc. I was very disappointed. I heard nothing of the grace and power of God.

A temperate and prudent leader has his act together. He understands that the grace of God is behind his abilities. He is calm in a crisis and able to view it from the perspective of a sovereign God.

How Do You Handle Circumstances?

Things change. Nothing remains the same. Things today are changing more rapidly than ever before. Change puts pressure on us. Paul, in 1 Timothy 3:2, refers to a quality called "respectable." The Greek word is our word for the universe, *cosmos*, It refers to the arrangement of things. The English word cosmetics is based on it—the arrangement of things on the face!

So a respectable leader is well-arranged. His mind is organized and he does not feel swamped by life's pressures and circumstances. He thrives on them. He doesn't cop out of responsibilities, but rather he faces them head-on.

A leader's desk is often a reflection of his leadership (Ouch! That remark hurt a little!). I guess it's OK to have your desk cluttered if you know where everything is that you need. However, to me that condition is convicting! I find that a clean desk at the end of the day (when possible) is a mark of good leadership. Don't put things off—deal with them today, if possible. You'll sleep better!

How Do Leaders React to People?

Five words in 1 Timothy 3:2,3 suggest the manner in which leaders should react to people. They are: hospitable, able to teach, gentle, not pugnacious, and uncontentious.

To be hospitable means loving strangers or guests—at work as well as at home. Hospitable refers to a person who is open to people, desiring to minister in some way. Leaders who are cold and aloof do not make good spiritual leaders. We need to be warm and friendly to all.

I was reminded of this recently when a man said to me that he really liked teaching school; it was the students who bothered him!

Able to teach refers to the way we communicate. It is used only one other time in the Bible, in 2 Timothy 2:24. The context there clearly shows that this is the quality of one who presents God's Word in a nonthreatened, objective, patient, and loving manner. The best way to identify this trait is when others disagree with you. If you jump all over them, condemning them or their viewpoint with great hostility (using spiritual words, of course!), then you are not manifesting the ability to teach. You yourself are not teachable. Every person is our teacher (even if we learn what not to do!). We need to be patient and loving at all times.

To be gentle is the opposite of being quick-tempered or contentious. It refers to one who is patient and forbearing. There is a willingness to yield to the other person. Ask yourself the question, "When was the last time I gave in to another person's opinion or viewpoint?" Are you always right?

A pugnacious person is one who physically strikes another person because of loss of control. This person has an angry, violent temperament. This has no place in spiritual leadership.

We had to ask one of our leaders to step down from leadership because he physically struck his wife on more than one occasion. At first he was very defensive when confronted (often a sign of guilt), but when he knew we had the facts, he realized he had forfeited his right to leadership.

Uncontentious—you can't be a spiritual leader if you are continually fighting others, insisting on your own way and rights. Some of us do that with issues as well as people. We pound a point into the ground that others see as minor and unimportant. We fight for things that have no value except in our own eyes. A spiritual leader knows when to yield and when to stand for what's right.

27

All of these traits affect our relationships with people and our ability to serve as a spiritual leader. There may be weak moments when you fail in one of these; but, are they patterns in your life? They should be observable.

Bad Habits Can Destroy Your Leadership!

Two bad habits are listed in 1 Timothy 3 that a leader should avoid. God wouldn't have listed them if they were not important and serious problems.

A spiritual leader must avoid being addicted to wine. The text indicates that he is not to be "alongside of" wine. It can refer to a drunk, but drunkenness is always a sin in the Bible. It can also refer to one who sits beside the wine when he needs to trust in something to solve his problems or drown his sorrows. A spiritual leader must have his confidence in the Lord and must learn to face his problems, not run away from them.

Under the guise of Christian liberty, many believers today feel free to drink alcoholic beverages. They use the Bible to justify their desire to have a little wine. After all, wine was used in Bible times. It was the Oriental beverage. The problem with all of this is that the word for "wine" can be applied to wine in its various stages of fermentation. Some passages in the Bible (such as Prov. 23:29-35) condemn the usage of wine in certain stages.

Without ignoring the medicinal usage of wine (see 1 Tim. 5:23) or the particular situations that we must face in the exercise of Christian liberty (see 1 Cor. 10:27), let's ask ourselves a basic question that is really a matter of spiritual leadership: "Why do you want to partake in that which is questionable?" Don't you have the freedom as a believer to refrain from doing that which others may do in order to be more effective in your ministry for the Lord? Spiritual leaders should live

28

"above reproach." Maybe you can handle it and maybe you can't. But your leadership is a higher priority than your personal desires. Why indulge (even if limited to rare occasions) in that which is questionable at all?

I asked one of our deacons who was having a problem in this area what he would think if I had a drink once in awhile. He said that he would question my leadership as his pastor. How inconsistent! He had a double standard. He wanted to be a spiritual leader like his pastor, but his personal desires were getting in the way. He concluded that as a deacon it was OK, but for the pastors—No! He even used the Scriptures to prove his point, pointing out that the deacons were forbidden to take "much wine" (1 Tim. 3:8), and that meant he could have a drink or two at times. The deacon was a close friend of mine, and the conclusion of this whole matter was that he saw his desire for wine as a hindrance to his spiritual leadership. He made a decision to get it out of his life. I have noticed a tremendous difference in his commitment to Christ ever since. It may seem like a small thing to you, but it does affect our spiritual leadership.

The second bad habit is the love of money. One without this habit has no ambition to be rich nor is impressed by great wealth. Money does not control his decisions. He is contented in this area (see 1 Tim. 6:6-10) and recognizes the tremendous heartaches and problems that can happen in the life of one controlled by the love of money.

One of my friends in the ministry lost his leadership over the love he had for money and what money can buy. "Things" became more important than people in his life. He always wanted a nicer car, a bigger house, and a larger salary. It was embarrassing at times to talk with him because these things so dominated his conver-

29

sation. I was not surprised when he left the ministry.

Recognizing a spiritual leader is the responsibility of God's people. Believers must be careful when they choose leaders. The standards of God's Word should be carefully observed. Always check a person's life over a period of time—never decide on the spur of a moment. Look for patterns, not moments of weakness. Above all, pray for God's wisdom and direction.

Leader's Checklist

1. Is there a continual desire in your heart for leadership? Describe it in a sentence or two.

2. Are you a new believer?

3. Are you devoted to your marital partner without any hesitation? Describe your feelings.

4. Do your children respond to your leadership? Why or why not?

5. Are you stable in difficult situations? Think of some recent examples.

6. Are you humble in evaluating your talents and gifts?

7. Do circumstances overwhelm you?

8. Are you patient with people or do they irritate you? List people who imitate you and try to understand why. How can you change your approach?

9. Do you yield to others or must you always be right?

10. Are you willing to give up questionable things in order to be a leader? List some pastimes, things, etc., you have given up or which you are willing to give up.

PART II

COMMUNICATION: DO PEOPLE KNOW WHAT YOU ARE SAYING?

YOU MUST COMMUNICATE WITH EVERYONE!

It was a staff memo that I sent out. It was simple—just the facts. We were planning a staff retreat for a couple of days at Palm Springs. I tried to state clearly the details about place, cost, time, etc., and that the church would pay part of the cost for everyone. I learned once again that those "inter-office memos" have a way of confusing and even irritating people! That memo was so misunderstood it resulted in several phone calls and many private conversations that consumed hours of time explaining the details that should have been clear in the memo. Oh well. You can't win them all!

Communication is the name of the game! It's not an option or a creative alternative—it's an essential for good leadership! Without communication, leadership cannot exist.

Communication is not merely the ability to talk. It is not merely saying the right words at the right time. You can do all of that and still not communicate. People often read your "spirit" (attitude) more than your lips. They seem to study the way you are saying something to find out why you are saying it or how important it is.

The way people respond to your communication is

often a barometer of your effectiveness in communicating. If you communicate properly, you should expect to see results. Those results should be in your mind before you start to communicate. It doesn't happen by talking a lot. Some leaders hope by their much talk that people will get the message. Ecclesiastes 5:7 says, "In many words there is emptiness."

We communicate with one another verbally and nonverbally. Even a simple glance or facial expression communicates a great deal to others. You might say that communication is a continuous process of life; life does not function apart from it. Every day and in every way we are communicating, whether good or bad. Leadership that does not pay attention to the importance of communication does so to its own hurt.

The larger the organization, the more pressing the problem of communicating with everyone becomes. Great numbers of people complicate the communication process. But, if all those people are to be involved in any task or project, then each must receive communication as to what they are to do and how it is to be accomplished and when it should be done.

In order to solve the problem of communicating to large numbers of people, organizations have designed levels of communication or responsibility. The main leader will delegate (if he is wise) responsibility to other leaders (or managers) to communicate with people under their area of responsibility. It is possible to conceive as many levels as necessary in order to limit the number of people that any one person must communicate with. If there are 40 people involved in a given task and they desire to limit the number of people to whom one person would communicate to just three people, how many levels of communication would there be? (Don't you just love riddles?) The answer? Just three levels. One leader would communicate to three others on the first level (total = 4); the three leaders would each communicate to three others (total = 9); the nine would communicate to three people each (total = 27), and all 40 would get the message (you hope). That would be far more communicative than if one leader would try to reach all 39 others by himself!

Understanding Levels of Communication

Communication began with God Himself. The Father was communicating with the Son, the Son with the Spirit, etc., before the world and man were ever created. Man learned about communication from God because God first communicated to man. He did this initially by what He made—the universe. Psalm 19:1-3 tells us that the universe is speaking all the time. It communicates to us about the greatness of God.

God also spoke directly to man in various ways (see Heb. 1:1,2) and communicated with a complete and final revelation in the Person of Jesus Christ. Today, the major way in which God is communicating to man is through the Bible.

Since the greatest communicator that ever lived is God Himself, it would be wise if the spiritual leader spent some time studying God's communication to man. Here are a few examples to get you started:

God always spoke the truth. He never lied.

God spoke with authority because of who He is.

God used various methods to communicate with men.

God told men what He wanted them to do in great detail.

God told men what results to expect.

God spoke with love and compassion.

God told men why He wanted them to do what He said. It was always for their good and His glory.

Well, the list could go on and on. We can learn much from God about how to communicate.

A spiritual leader will suffer greatly if he does not experience the level of communication that we call prayer, communication between man and God. There is a sense in which our communication with other people is limited when we do not communicate with God in prayer. Prayer was the first priority in Moses' job description. To talk with God is more important than talking with anyone else.

There will be times when the only way we can communicate to other people what we want to say is after prayer. There is a wonderful example of this in the book of Nehemiah. He was faced with the role of leadership; it was desperately needed due to the condition of things (see Neh. 1:2,3) in Jerusalem. The first thing Nehemiah did was to pray (see Neh. 1:4-11). When the king asked Nehemiah what his request was, Nehemiah again prayed (see Neh. 2:4). In order to communicate effectively, Nehemiah sought God's help. Do you?

Other levels of communication exist between husband and wife, parent and child, friends, at the marketplace, through TV and radio, etc. Life is filled with communication.

Leaders cannot lead effectively without communicating at all levels. You cannot isolate yourself from the people you are to lead.

Leaders are constantly subjected to communicating with the group as well as with the individual. The leader is communicating to a group of people, or a group of people are trying to communicate with the leader. The group can be a small committee of three people or a crowd of thousands. In communicating with a group, there are two basic problems: one deals with the individual's authority over the group; the other deals with the group's authority over the individual. This is an extremely important matter in most organizations (including churches!).

If the individual is subservient to the group (whether committee, board, or total organization), the communication problem grows, as well as the difficulties in terms of flexibility, change, implementation of ideas, etc. Many churches in America are suffering from this problem. Instead of leadership residing in the pastor, it often resides in a board or committee. That particular style of organization is usually a hindrance to growth. A group is incapable of making decisions quickly when needed, and communication must filter through varying viewpoints and ideas.

Our church used to be operated by the concept of a board of people representing the many ministries of the church. Communication was slow and tedious in this concept. It took much time to accomplish things. Authority moved from one person to another, and decisions were not made when needed.

After these people spent time studying the Scriptures, they changed the organizational structure and put the leadership in the hands of a few leaders, the elders, rather than in a large body of people, the board. Growth soon took place in a way the people had not seen before.

However, putting leadership in the hands of only one person can be dangerous. If that person responsible for making decisions has a bad character, then the whole organization will suffer. Proverbs 29:2 says, "When the righteous increase, the people rejoice, but when a wicked man rules, people groan." Also, if that leader does not seek the wisdom of others, whether committee or board, that organization will not succeed. Proverbs 15:22 reminds us, "With many counselors they succeed." Many para-church organizations have been started by individuals who, in turn, appointed a board of directors to which they had to be accountable. This in and of itself is not a bad thing, but it becomes a problem when the board is the chief decision-making instrument for the carrying on of that organization's goals.

Groups do not make good leaders; individuals do! If you want someone to lead, then let him lead. Don't keep telling him how to lead! If you don't believe he is qualified or doing the job required, then remove him and get someone who can do the job.

The key word in the relationship between an individual and a group is *balance*. The individual must recognize the importance of the group in terms of ideas, suggestions, and opinions. There is importance and weight behind decisions that are recognized by a group, even though an individual made that decision. The group's role must be supportive. The group must recognize the role of the individual as the leader. He must be free to lead. It is also wise if the leader is chosen by the group or organization. The leader will then sense overall responsibility and accountability to that group or organization. The chief role of the group is to employ the services of the leader and support him in the decisions, goals, and objectives that are being carried out.

The frustration of being the leader but not having the authority to act was mine many years ago. I was associated with an organization whose board hired me, but placed me in the role of carrying out their decisions. I felt trapped and discouraged. I knew then and there that their system was wrong. The growth and development of the organization was hindered. The board did not face the problems on a day-to-day basis nor did they understand the needs.

Having faced the situation of being a leader but not being free to lead many times since, I have observed certain principles that affect communication between the individual and the group.

How can an individual best communicate to a group?

• Establish the importance of each member of the group in relationship to what you desire to communicate.

• Do not reflect attitudes of superiority over the group (in the way you talk, or where you sit, or how you dress, or how you greet them). As a member of a board of trustees for a growing educational system I noticed how often the chairman of the board would adjust to what the other members of the board were wearing. He usually started with a suit and tie. If the board members showed up without coats, he removed his. If they had sport shirts on, he removed his coat and tie. He was a wise leader. He wanted to identify with the group to which he was communicating.

• Maintain eye contact with each member of the group if possible. If you don't, they will wonder why!

• Learn to use plural pronouns, "we" and "our," instead of singular ones, "I" and "mine." One leader irritated myself and others on the committee we were serving by constantly referring to himself. As far as he was concerned, we were totally unnecessary. He definitely had an "I" problem!

• Ask questions of members in the group that indicate you need their help and support. The way you ask the question is also very important. Instead of saying, "You do agree with what I'm saying, don't you?" try this one, "What do you think about it, John?" Or, "Is this the wise thing to do in your opinion?" Or, "Is there a better way that we can do this?"

• Allow members of the group freedom to express different ideas and opinions. You can't really do this if you rebuke them for what they express, or if their position in the organization, or their relationship with you as the leader would be jeopardized. Can others disagree with you and still be your friend?

• Learn to admit your mistakes in the presence of the group and to apologize sincerely when things go wrong or do not turn out the way you expected. One of the toughest assignments I have as a leader is to admit I made a mistake (especially if it's a big one!). I used to think that admitting you failed is a sign of weakness. It can be if you always fail! But, admitting failure in the midst of success is a key to good leadership. Learn to be open and honest before others. They'll love you for it (or at least fall over backwards out of shock!).

• Never blame the group for the failure of the organization. Accept the blame yourself (after all, you are the leader—ultimately, it really is your fault!). A pastor told me one day that the real problem in his church was his deacons. They were the reason why his church was not growing. As long as he holds that view, his church will remain stagnant and unresponsive. The problem is in the heart of that pastor. He refuses to accept the blame for the failure of his church to grow, but instead he committed a "Freudian slip" by blaming others (a sure sign you're guilty of something!).

• In small groups, call people by their first names, unless they are very much older than you are or of higher position. In large groups, use careful discretion, especially when you do not know the person so well. It is especially tragic in communication when you cannot call someone by his right name. I was counseling one day with a longtime and trusted friend. In the midst of a very important sentence I called him by someone else's name. I couldn't believe I did that! Was I ever embarrassed! He felt at that moment my lack of care for him as a person. Every one of us enjoys hearing someone call our name.

• Begin and end with prayer. Always manifest a continual trust and dependence upon God. A group will respond to an individual better if the individual begins the conversation with prayer. In the opening prayer, ask for wisdom and guidance. In the closing prayer, express thanks and praise, regardless of the outcome.

One of the more difficult forms of communication is when a group must communicate to the individual. This occurs in the life of a church from time to time as individuals must be confronted by two or three (see Matt. 18:15-17) people, by a committee or board, or with organizational problems. Here are some helpful hints on handling this problem.

• Do not isolate that person from the group in the seating arrangement. I have never enjoyed sitting alone at the end of a table while several others sat on the other end. This will cause poor communication. Sometimes people use this seating arrangement to establish authority. That is really not necessary. It suggests an insecure authority.

• Each member of the group should take time to greet that person, if possible. This creates warmth immediately. The person will appreciate the concern of each member of the group to personally greet him.

• Do not try to overpower the individual by the authority of the group. It will be very difficult to communicate effectively if the individual believes you are trying to put him down by the importance or authority of the group. I experienced this problem once while appearing before a missions board. They continued to impress me with their authority, making me wonder whether or not my viewpoint would ever be heard. I felt on the defensive and had a difficult time communicating. I realize the problem was my attitude, but I also learned a lesson from that experience that I try to apply in my ministry

40

now. A group should never try to overwhelm or impress an individual with their authority.

• Establish the importance of the individual. The group should do what they can to manifest their desire for the individual's point of view. They must be sincere. The group should be willing to listen to the individual's point of view with respect.

• Be careful about manifesting a critical spirit of an individual's ideas, decisions, or opinions without first hearing his side. It seems that there are three sides to every issue: your view, the other person's view, and the real truth. A critical spirit can cut off communication.

• Seek to help the individual by what you say. Prepare yourself mentally for this before the discussion ever starts. Ask yourself the question, "What can I say that will really help and build up this person?"

• Unless something is morally wrong with what is said, always be willing to support the ideas of the individual, even when those ideas may not coincide with what you were thinking. A kind word like, "I had not thought about that," can really encourage another person. Or say something like, "I really appreciate hearing your side of this matter." Everyone likes to hear, "That's a great idea!" You may not agree with the idea, but at least acknowledge its value.

• Do not try to communicate an idea to the individual by talking to someone else in the group. Always look the individual in the eye and speak directly to him.

• Seek to encourage the individual by identifying with the loneliness he feels. So often groups fail to appreciate the position of the individual who faces the group.

• Begin and end with prayer.

Does Everyone Know What to Know?

One of the fundamental problems in communication

is inadequate information. Everyone needs to receive communication, but often something is missing. Ask yourself, "Does my communication tell what to do, how to do it, and when it must be done?" Be brief but be complete. Say it concisely, but make sure you've said enough.

It is hard to expect what you do not inspect. In communication, it is wise to check up on what you communicated. Do it sweetly, however. Don't make people think that you don't trust them!

One of the greatest ways to communicate with everyone is to say "thank you." A word of appreciation will greatly help your next communication. Do it personally and not in front of others. You want them to know that you are not showing appreciation just so others will think well of you. A little note from you saying "thanks" goes a long way toward building effective communication.

Leader's Checklist
1. Do you communicate daily with the Lord in prayer?
2. How many levels of communication in your ministry do you need to communicate with?
3. Are you open to people? Can they disagree with you without affecting their relationship with you?
4. Do you appreciate the viewpoints of others? How do you show it?
5. Do you look people in the eye and speak directly to them?
6. Can you apologize in front of others?
7. Do you take the blame for the failures in your organization?
8. Are you open to new ideas? Can you change your viewpoint?
9. Do you tell people "thank you"?

WHAT MAKES PEOPLE LISTEN?

One Sunday morning after preaching, a man came up to me in the presence of several people and began to point out what was wrong with what I had just preached. He did not introduce himself. I had never seen him before. He interrupted another person I was talking to. He talked quite loudly. He was angry and intolerant of others' feelings. He was judgmental without hearing the facts. He misunderstood what I said (or, I misunderstood what I said!). He used bad grammar. It was time for lunch and I was hungry. My family was waiting in the car. Needless to say, we had a communication problem!

It doesn't matter what you say or how loudly you talk, some people are not listening. Communication is not one-sided. One speaks, but another must listen. Listening is a lost art. Most people are waiting for the other person to stop talking so that they can talk. Listening sometimes is nothing more than endurance! No wonder there is little communication!

I sat on the platform with a group of very distinguished people on one occasion and listened to an eloquent speaker talk for two hours to an audience of over 2,000 people. A friend of mine remarked to me afterwards that the speaker should be called "birdbath" because he was so shallow! He said nothing, but he said it well! People were obviously bored and irritated. I tried my best to discern what he was talking about. He seemed in love with his voice and his vocabulary. What a tragedy, I thought.

Why People Are Not Listening

What are some of the common barriers to communication? Why do people not listen at times? What is the problem?

You talk too much! This is a very common problem. We have all met people who seem to believe that people will understand what they are trying to say if they use a lot of words. But Solomon in Ecclesiastes says, "Let your words be few" (5:2) and the "voice of a fool" comes "through many words" (5:3), and "in many words there is emptiness" (5:7).

There are two problems to face if one is talking too much. One is the problem of remembering. People listening can easily forget some of what you say because there is so much to remember! Two, one can easily become bored with a great volume of words and mentally fall asleep! (Some people do that literally!) Many people cannot be content with sharing the important points because they sincerely believe that the "details" are what makes it interesting. Remember, you may think that all the details are interesting, but that doesn't mean that they are or that they are to the person to whom you are communicating. Learn to be brief, concise, and to the point. Try to state what you want to say in your first sentence. (It may save you lots of time and embarrassment!)

You don't say enough. We have all had the experience of receiving some sort of communication from someone who did not give all the facts or clear enough instruction for us to do anything about what he shared. It can be very frustrating. Sometimes you wind up blaming yourself for not understanding or being able to read between the lines.

If you are a concerned communicator, you will ask questions of the people you are talking with to ascertain whether or not they have received enough information to be able to act upon what you shared.

You use language that's too eloquent. We are not against good vocabulary nor the right use of words in a given sentence. However, it is well known that people who try to impress others with their eloquence or style of speaking are actually putting up another barrier to communication. The late Dr. Bob Jones, Sr. had a classic statement in this regard when he said, "It is better to say 'I seen it' than 'I saw it' if you really saw something, than to say 'I saw it' when you didn't see it at all!"

A leader will structure his message to the level of his hearer's understanding. He will take into consideration not only his audience's level of education but also their cultural background.

When we use eloquence for effect, people begin to believe that we are proud and more interested in impressing them with our vocabulary than sincerely wanting to communicate with them.

You make derogatory remarks. A person can use these remarks to try to impress another person with his authority or knowledge or opinion, especially in comparison to another's point of view. We often use labels to accomplish this. We may say that a person is a "radical" and thus hope to cut off people's support of him. We may say that an issue is too "controversial" and thus

45

avoid dealing with it. We might attack a person's views by saying, "Well, what do you expect from a man like that!" Often we question a person's motivation in the presence of others in order to diminish the importance of what that person said. It goes like this: "I know what he said, but if you really knew why he said it you would know why it is wrong."

There are all kinds of tricks people use in order to reduce the effectiveness of what someone else says or does. It is pride that causes it, and our foolish reasoning that believes we will look better in the eyes of others if we put people down. Ephesians 4:29 says, "Let no unwholesome word proceed from your mouth, but only such a word as is good for edification according to the need of the moment, that it may give grace to those who hear." Our desire should be to build others up, not tear them down.

You exaggerate. There are different reasons why people exaggerate. Sometimes we do it to make ourselves look better than we are. Other times we do it just so people will listen to us and think that what we are saying is important. Sometimes we do it in order to cover up some wrong or mistake in our lives. Very few people want to admit that exaggerations are often nothing but lies, or at least attempts to deceive people by distorting the facts. Consider the several ways we do this and recognize that they are all barriers to communication:

(1) We make small incidents seem big. Some like to call this "making a mountain out of a molehill." Relationships among church members are often hurt because of this problem in communication. Suppose one of your teenagers did not come home one night due to being stranded with automobile difficulties in another city or town. Before too long, the rumor is out that your teen-

46

ager did not come home because of immorality; his reputation is destroyed by careless exaggeration of what really happened. We have all had examples of such stories and have seen how they can be blown up by people who delight in relating them to others. This kind of gossip without careful knowledge of the facts is dangerous and harmful. Love does not rejoice in someone else's tragedies or problems, nor does it seek to parade them to others. Also, when you become guilty of making small incidents seem bigger than they are, you lose credibility with people and your communication is greatly affected.

(2) We over-generalize. This is a common problem among people in communication and we must recognize how serious it is. It is making general statements about things or people that usually contain the word "all" or "every." One example: "*Everyone* knows that about him." Now, we *all* know that is not true! (See how I attempted to persuade you with the word "all"!)

Another example: "*Everyone* is doing it." Many young people are influenced by that kind of logic! The fact is, everyone is not doing it. The usage of "everyone" is an exaggeration used by people to get others to agree with them about what they are saying.

Another example: "*Everything* has gone wrong today." Maybe a great deal has gone wrong from your perspective, but others may not feel the same way about it as you do. We often try to make people accept our viewpoint of things by such over-generalizations. Eventually it will catch up with us, and people who think for themselves will begin to question our trustworthiness as communicators.

(3) We make cause and effect statements. We use these *all* the time (There I go again!), or at least they seem to be used a great deal by people. In theology, we

47

might illustrate with this statement: "Calvinism leads to dead orthodoxy," or "Arminianism leads to liberalism." Neither statement is true, but it might be true in some cases. These are exaggerations. "Where there's smoke, there's fire." That little saying is often used to prove a point about someone's actions. If they do one thing, we figure automatically that they are going to do another. This is dangerous reasoning and bad communication. "All charismatics are very emotional people." The idea here is that if you become a charismatic (theologically) you will become more emotional than if you were not one. However, there are many non-charismatics who are very emotional people, and charismatics who seem to be unemotional and more academic and intellectual in their personality traits. Again, the cause and effect exaggeration is used by people to prove a point that they personally believe but which cannot be established by facts.

(4) We think only in terms of either/or. Everything seems black or white to those who use this type of reasoning. Something is either right or it is wrong. A person is either a friend or an enemy. The trouble is that life is not that simple. There are "grey areas" and "twilight zones" where we simply cannot draw such hard and fast conclusions. We might say, "You're either a Calvinist or an Arminian—which are you?" If the person answers, "Well, I think I'm somewhere in between —like a Calminian!" then we who like things black or white will become critical and judgmental of this answer and probably accuse the person of being a "compromiser." People who aspire to be leaders must be very careful about communicating this kind of attitude. You will convince people around you that they must be 100 percent for you or they are 100 percent against you. But the truth may be that they are 90 percent for you, but 10

percent of the time they disagree with you. A wise leader allows for more flexibility than to make exaggerated either/or statements.

(5) We misuse statistics. You have heard it said, "Figures don't lie, but liars figure!" Many of us in areas of spiritual leadership are all too aware of this problem. Statistics are used by people to prove whether their efforts are being mightily used of God or not. However, it is relatively easy to distort the facts a little without lying. A simple example would be in the use of graphs— is it vertical or horizontal? What are the numbers on the graph that you are comparing your statistics with? For instance: A graph that has divisions of 10 (like 10, 20, 30, etc.) can show a greater growth than one with divisions of 100 (like 100, 200, 300, etc.). Also, when we use statistics, we often speak of the "average." But, what is "average"? What does that mean? Often the problem deals with what is not evident in the statistics. It is not so much what we show, but what we don't show. A church might argue that 50 percent of a certain Sunday School class is involved in evangelism. That is all good and impressive. But, suppose the class that is chosen is the smallest in numbers, and there are 20 classes that have larger attendances. And, suppose that when the church evaluates all of the classes, less than 5 percent are involved in evangelism! The question behind the use of statistics is why the information is being shared. Is it to impress or to inform? Is it to be proud of what was accomplished or to be motivated to do better? A church may state that it had 100 decisions last year, but may fail to mention that only 2 of those are now members of the church and growing in their faith. It is very easy to exaggerate a situation with the use of statistics, and leaders must be careful here in terms of their communication with people. If the facts are distorted or if the

complete picture is not given, people will begin to question your motivations.

You appeal to authority. A very common barrier to communication is appealing to some authority (rather than God or the Scriptures) in order to substantiate what we are saying or our right to say it. When we study the reasons why people believe anything, we usually discover three sources are involved: direct experience, reasoning with certain facts, or acceptance of authority. However, when an appeal to some authority is used to prove a point or increase the chances that what the speaker says is reliable, we need to ask certain basic questions like "Is the authority competent in that subject?" Or, "Is that authority reliable?" We must also ask, "Is that authority supported by other reliable sources?" We must determine how that quoted authority was supporting his point. We must ask, "What was the context of that remark?" "Is the authority prejudiced in that area?" It is easy to use this kind of appeal, especially with those who have died. No one wants to question the reliability of some person who died in a previous era and whose name represents solid Christian leadership or dedication in the past. But remember, people are people! Great leaders and authorities in the past also had certain problems and hang-ups. We must be very discerning in our use of authority. Some of us are compulsive "name-droppers." We think that by mentioning certain famous people we are substantiating the validity of our remarks. The truth may be that we are causing people to wonder why we do that. It often becomes a serious barrier in communication.

You beg the question. Simply stated, this means that we assume truth or error without proof. Leaders (sometimes because of their position) will do this often because they are used to being the authority. Sometimes we "beg the question" by arguing in circles. An example of such reasoning from the arguments of evolution: a person may ask, "How do we know how old the fossils are in this particular stratum?" The answer might be, "By the stratum in which they appear." Then, you might ask, "But how do we know how old the stratum is?" Answer: "By the fossils that appear in it." Obviously, this is "reasoning in a circle."

The common problem is that we assume the truth of a proposition that "everybody" seems to know or at least accept (for one reason or another). We sometimes use emotional words in our sentences to emphasize our point, even though we have no proof of what we are saying. Things like, "I *really* believe this with *all my heart*." It is commendable that you believe something that strongly, but you could possibly be wrong! Be sure the facts are clear.

All of these barriers to communication are experienced by people who work together day after day. It will help your relationships with others when you recognize what they are and learn to avoid them.

Why People Listen

It's one thing to talk about the problems, it's quite another thing to have solutions! What kind of qualities make others listen to your communication? In my experience, there are at least five major qualities that are necessary for effective communication to take place.

You must be honest and be able to tell the truth at all times. Sometimes it is not appropriate or necessary to reveal all that we know, but we should never lie. Sometimes we have to say, "I'm sorry, but I am not able to share that information at this time." Breakdowns in communication happen when there is a lack of honesty. Proverbs 14:25 says, "A truthful witness saves lives, but he who speaks lies is treacherous." Verse 5 of the same chapter states, "A faithful witness will not lie, but a false witness speaks lies." Proverbs 12:19 adds, "Truthful lips will be established forever, but a lying tongue is only for a moment."

A lady shared with me the difficulty she and her husband were having in communicating with each other. It all started when she learned that he had lied to her about a certain matter. She could no longer trust him. His confession to her was not complete, and so once again, she did not trust him. It was hard to listen to him. She found it difficult to talk to him under any circumstances. His lack of honesty led him to a lack of good communication.

We must respect other people's confidence. Things that are shared in confidence must be kept that way. Leadership will diminish in the eyes of others when it is guilty of gossip. Proverbs 11:13 says, "He who goes about as a talebearer reveals secrets, but he who is trustworthy conceals a matter." Proverbs 17:9 adds, "He who covers a transgression seeks love, but he who repeats a matter separates intimate friends."

But how do you handle a situation where someone tells you to keep this in strict confidence and tell no one else? First of all, do not promise it unless you intend to keep that confidence. On certain occasions it might be better to say, "I will do my best to keep it, but I must first hear what it is to determine whether anyone else should know about it. I do promise to tell you if there is someone else who should know about this." This is important in counseling. What is shared must be told to another party if that party is involved and reconciliation is needed.

Secondly, you must determine whether what a person is going to share with you is gossip or not. Not only

52

should we not gossip ourselves, but we should not get into the habit of listening to someone else who is gossiping. Be careful what you share with others!

We must be open. If people are going to respond to us in personal communication they must see an openness about us that allows them to share without fear of what we may think, say, or do. Many subordinates will not share with those in authority over them because they believe they will suffer in the process.

One of our staff members was involved in a matter that necessitated his telling me about it. He kept it from me for some time until I found out about it from someone else. When I confronted him with it, he said that he didn't want to tell me about it because he thought it would affect his job. Now, that can be his problem as well as mine. It reminded me of the importance of openness. I must be open enough to fellow staff members so that they will feel free to discuss things with me without fear.

Effective communication is based upon the ability to listen. If people do not believe you listen to them, your leadership will diminish in their eyes. A part of the way in which people will evaluate this is by how many of their ideas and suggestions you eventually use. When a leader never uses any idea or suggestion someone else makes, or if he criticizes another person, people will visualize that leader as being closed and overconfident and worst of all, self-centered.

You must accept other people. People must believe that you accept them fully and unconditionally. A lack of acceptance is evident when you talk down to a person. You are judgmental of what a person has said or done, especially when you are not involved in the situation. Often, we give our opinions when they are not wanted or needed, an unwise practice.

When you show partiality, people sense that you do not accept them. God treats us all alike, and so should we in our relationships with others.

In a counseling situation I found a lady extremely hesitant about discussing her problems, even though that was her original purpose in coming to see me. She grew up in a home where the parents accepted her on the basis of how she performed. She became reluctant to share her problems lest people refuse to accept her when she wasn't performing as they expected. What a joy to tell her of God's unconditional love and total acceptance!

You must show love. More about this in a later chapter. Just one thing at this point about love and communication. If people do not believe that you sincerely love them or care about them as people, very little real communication will take place, lots of talk but little communication! First Corinthians 13:1 says, "If I speak with the tongues of men and of angels [that's communication!], but do not have love, I have become a noisy gong or a clanging cymbal [that's noise!]." Love will deepen the level of communication. Love enriches the response of the listener. Love sweetens the way things are said. Above all, love!

Leadership is not so much the ability you have as an individual to do great things by yourself, but rather your ability to get others to help you accomplish things. This takes good communication on a one-to-one basis. Talking with individuals before making crucial decisions is not only advisable but necessary for good leadership. Do not pull things on people without consulting with them privately. No surprises, please! Proverbs 15:22 says, "Without consultation, plans are frustrated, but with many counselors they succeed." Amen! Let's communicate!

Leader's Checklist

1. Do you talk too much, irritating people?

2. Do you say enough to tell people what to do, how to do it, and when it should be done?

3. Are you conscious of being eloquent, thinking that this will impress people?

4. Do you use derogatory remarks, putting people down in order to inflate your own importance?

5. Do you have a problem with exaggerations, trying to embellish things so people will respond better?

6. Do you make too much of small incidents?

7. Do you often appeal to others in authority to make people believe what you are saying?

8. Do you assume the truth of your statements without proving them?

9. Are you known by others as being truthful at all times?

10. Do you have a problem with gossip, or can you be trusted?

11. Do people feel free to talk with you without fear of what you may think, say, or do?

12. Do people believe that you accept and love them without conditions of performance on their part?

One way to answer the above questions is on a scale of 1 to 10. Score yourself, then ask a trusted friend or colleague to score you.

PART III

ABILITY: ARE YOU CAPABLE OF LEADING OTHER PEOPLE?

ARE YOU
ONE OF CHRIST'S
GIFTED LEADERS?

What kind of leaders do we need for the church today? Jesus is no longer here, but in heaven. He is building His church. He knows it needs leadership, so He designed four types. They are mentioned in Ephesians 4:11: apostles, prophets, evangelists, and pastor-teachers. Ephesians 4:7 calls them gifts.

Is it possible that after studying management principles and leadership techniques, learning everything there is to know, you might still fail in being a good leader? Of course! But why? Lots of reasons. One big one might deal with spiritual gifts. The question is, "Are you one of Christ's gifted leaders to the church?" And, "How do you know if you are one?"

Let's begin by asking what these gifted leaders are supposed to do. The Bible states in Ephesians 4:12 that the four gifted leaders are to be "equipping the saints for the work of service, to the building up of the body of Christ." Simple enough. But what does that mean? Equipping someone can be illustrated from the world of fishing. When fishermen in Bible times were mending their nets, the word "equipping" was used. The nets were being tied together so that the fish would not slip out. The term was also used when two pieces of material were joined together. Equipping means that you are putting people together so that they can do a great work.

Second Timothy 3:16,17 tells us that the Scriptures are designed to equip the man of God for every good work. Each believer can help to build up the Body of Christ (other believers) when he is equipped. He becomes equipped with the Scriptures.

The work that the believers do in order to build up others is called the "work of service." First Peter 4:10, 11 seems to indicate that this refers to the use of spiritual gifts. Every believer has at least one spiritual gift. In order to use it properly and effectively, he needs to be equipped with the knowledge of the Word of God. That assignment was given to the four gifted leaders of Ephesians 4:11. They are responsible to equip. The result will be that the Body of Christ will be built, both quantitatively, as well as qualitatively.

Many Christian leaders are frustrated in their jobs because they are doing things that do not reflect the kind of person God designed them to be. In other words, instead of working in the area of their gifts, they are trying to do things they were never equipped to do.

If you are presently serving as a leader in the ministry of the church, which one of the four gifted leaders are you? Are you an apostle? Prophet? Evangelist? Pastor-teacher? Where do you fit in?

Are You An Apostle?

Didn't Jesus have just 12 apostles? Yes. Then, how could a person today be an apostle? Easy! There were more apostles than just the Twelve special ones who walked with Jesus when He was here. Look at 1 Corinthians 15:5-7 where it says Christ appeared to the

Twelve, and then "to all the apostles." Here are the names of a few more apostles beside the Twelve: Paul—Galatians 1:1; Epaphroditus—Philippians 2:25 (translated "messenger"); Barnabas—Acts 14:4; Titus—2 Corinthians 8:23 (translated "messenger"); Silvanus and Timothy—1 Thessalonians 1:1, cf. 2:6; Andronicus and Junias—Romans 16:7; James (the Lord's brother)—Galatians 1:19.

What about the apostles being the foundation of the church? We're not building the foundation anymore, are we? Some apostles were used in a special way to write books of the Bible. To them, God gave special and direct communication. They are called "holy" apostles and prophets (Eph. 2:20; 3:5). The word holy means "separated" or "set apart." A certain group of apostles and prophets were set apart to write Scripture. No more need today for that kind of apostle or for the Twelve who walked with Jesus. The names of the Twelve will be special forever (cf. Matt. 19:28 and Rev. 21:14). The Scriptures are completed.

There were apostles who were not a part of the Twelve special friends of Jesus, nor did they write any Scripture. For example, Barnabas, Timothy, and Titus—what did they do? They were the missionaries of Bible times. They, like Paul, traveled from place to place planting churches and building up the new believers. They were responsible for leadership development in these new churches. That's why Paul told Timothy and Titus to ordain (or select) elders (bishops) in every church. That's the work of an apostle. See Acts 14:21-28 for a complete breakdown on what these apostles or church-planters were doing.

We still need apostles today. Maybe the word should be changed to identify with modern terminology, but they are still needed. With over two billion people in the world who have yet to hear the gospel of Christ, we still need the pioneer types. Do you have a desire to travel? Would you like the joy of building something from the bottom up? Do you like to start something, get it going, and then turn it over to others?

I had the joy of doing the work of an apostle or church-planter. It took me longer than the apostle Paul, but then that's understandable—I'm not the apostle Paul! I spent about three- and-a-half years establishing a church in Columbus, Ohio. It was loads of fun (as well as some heartaches)! God blessed, people were saved, leaders developed, and the church grew. Its present leadership is doing so much better with that ministry than I ever did, but I was there when it all started. What a joy! What a privilege!

Apostles, church-planters, pioneer missionaries—call them whatever you want! But, we still need them! Are you interested? Has God placed that desire in your heart? Does it stay with you most of the time? What's holding you back?

Are You a Prophet?

If you ask the question, "Are you a prophet?" in some circles it is a joke. If you think of a prophet as a predictor of the future, then we certainly don't need them today. The Bible is sufficient to tell us about the future and how things are going to turn out. But the idea of a prophet as one who foretells the future is a product of the Middle Ages. The word prophet means "to speak before." Not only can it refer to one who speaks about a thing before it happens, but in its common usage in Bible times it can refer to one who speaks before a crowd of people. In ancient society, a prophet was a public speaker. Prophets were what we call preachers. In the church at Antioch (see Acts 13:1) there were both prophets and

61

teachers. The prophets were proclaimers of God's truth.

God told prophets what to say. There was a sense of urgency and importance about their message. Aaron was a prophet, and under God's direction he was simply a mouthpiece for Moses (see Exod. 7:1). Some prophets in the New Testament predicted the future (Agabus— see Acts 11:28), while others simply relayed a message that brought encouragement and strength to believers (Judas and Silas—see Acts 15:32).

The purpose of prophesying was to speak to men for edification, exhortation, and consolation (see 1 Cor. 14:3). The gift was also used to bring conviction to the nonbeliever (see 1 Cor. 14:24).

I overheard a lady say when referring to a recent guest speaker in our church, "He's a preacher, but not much of a teacher!" I have also heard that in reverse, "He's a teacher, but no preacher!" Perhaps we should look to the matter of gifts before we become too critical of the different kinds of spiritual leaders. If prophesying is related to forthtelling rather than foretelling, then it might parallel today's references to preaching, rather than predictors of the future.

If the prophet's ministry was to be a public speaker, to speak before the crowds, then we could easily visualize the need for prophets as well as pastor-teachers in the ministry of the local church. It might be possible to conclude that the larger a church grows (larger the crowd), the more necessary it is to have the "preacher-type" who can communicate effectively with the large crowd. "Teacher-types" do well in smaller groups and classroom situations. Both preachers and teachers are needed. There is a sense in which a man who preaches should also teach, and one who teaches should also preach. One is concerned with content (teacher) and the other with application (preacher). One cares about what is communicated (teacher), and the other (preacher) with how it is communicated.

It is my opinion (not dogmatic, just thinking about it!) that we have both types in the ministry of our church and among our pastoral staff. We have men of the Word who are excellent teachers (both young and old) who have difficulty communicating before a large crowd of people. It affects their whole presentation. We have others who love to "preach" to the large crowd, whether in the pulpit or at the beach, or in a college environment with hundreds of students. Some seem gifted as communicators and motivators, while others are outstanding in study, research and teaching content. There is room for both in the ministry of the church. It is time that we recognize gifts. There are enormous differences in people and ministries that need biblical explanation.

Are You an Evangelist?

Only one man is called an evangelist in the Bible—Philip (see Acts 21:8). He was one of the original seven of Acts 6, chosen to help the apostles in handling the distribution of food to needy widows. He was a godly man and faithful in ministry in the Jerusalem church. However, God led him into a ministry of evangelism in Samaria (see Acts 8) as well as in other places. He eventually settled down in Caesarea where he raised his family.

What did Philip do? He preached Christ. He told people about Jesus. He shared with many in Samaria as well as with one Ethiopian eunuch who was returning from Jerusalem in his chariot. An evangelist is a teller of the good news. His greatest joy is found in telling folks how to become a Christian and leading them to a knowledge of Christ. Philip also baptized those who responded to his message. After all, that is a vital part of the Great Commission of our Lord (see Matt. 28:19, 20).

We have three men on our staff who I believe are evangelists. There are lots more among the members of our church. I have observed a few things about these particular men over the years. They do not enjoy sitting at a desk all day unless they are talking to someone about Christ. They are people-oriented. They love to be around people. They love to talk with people wherever they are. They are outgoing and their zeal is contagious. They do not feel at home when studying or doing research. They must push themselves to study and teach. Everyone must study the Bible, but to them it does not come easily. They love the Word and use it constantly, but doing a word study for hours in an office is not their thing! If they go for weeks without seeing someone come to Christ they are depressed and burdened. Their greatest desire is to see people come to know Christ. They are great examples to all of us in how to share our faith. I have also observed that they lead more people to Christ than staff members with other gifts.

What about you? Are you an evangelist? Do you desire to talk with people about the Lord? Do you feel discouraged when you do not have that opportunity? Do you love people? Would you rather talk to a person than work at a desk? These questions and many more should be asked of every person who believes he is gifted in evangelism. All believers are responsible to witness, but not all are gifted by God. Those with the gift of evangelist can be of great help in training others how to share their faith in Christ.

It is also important to keep evangelists free to do their ministry. A layman in our church who seems gifted in evangelism was greatly discouraged one day. He was told by another Christian that if he did not disciple those he led to Christ, he was not obedient to Christ. He told me about his job and the time he had available. He shared with me that during the previous three months he had led eight people to Christ. He had no time to disciple them nor did he feel that desire. I went to the person who told him to disciple his converts, and explained that those gifted in evangelism should be kept free to do that ministry and that others could help in the discipling of these converts—namely, him! He saw the point, and began immediately to help his brother to meet the needs of those new converts. We are all needed in the Body of Christ, but our gifts are different. We should not try to make everyone feel as we do about ministering. Recognize the differences and seek to build up one another.

Are You a Pastor-Teacher?

Are pastors the same as teachers, and is every pastor responsible to be a teacher? Could not some be teachers and not be pastors? Because gifts are different both in type and in the way they are used, we must be careful about being too dogmatic about the use of gifts. However, Ephesians 4:11 does make pastors the same as teachers. The Greek construction of that verse demands that there are four gifted leaders mentioned, not five. In that context at least, a pastor is the same as a teacher, and a teacher the same as a pastor.

A pastor is a shepherd, responsible to provide food and protection for his sheep. In order to provide food, he must be a teacher of God's Word. Not every pastor has the spiritual gift of teaching mentioned in Romans 12:7; but every pastor has the responsibility to teach. Not every elder in a church is a pastor-teacher (see 1 Tim. 5:17), but those who are pastors are to be teachers.

Several years ago a young man in our ministry felt

that God was calling him to leadership as a pastor-teacher. I encouraged him to begin his ministry in the local church where he could be observed and his desires and gifts could be confirmed by others. Each class or Bible study he got involved with as a teacher declined in attendance. People were gracious, but frankly, he could not teach. Finally, he came to me about this matter. We talked it over and discussed the importance of spiritual gifts. It is important to recognize what gifts we don't have so that we can begin to concentrate on gifts we do have. He got the point! He has a fine ministry now, but not as a pastor-teacher. I have often wondered what kind of frustration and discouragement would be in his life now if I had tried to persuade him to be a pastor-teacher in spite of what his ministry in that area had proven to be!

The wisdom of putting the two words of pastor and teacher together to describe the ministry of this gifted leader is obvious. Some teachers have no desire to minister to people. They do not have a "shepherd's heart." Some who have the understanding and compassion of a pastor, do not desire to teach nor do any study of God's Word. Balance is so important.

A pastor-teacher's goals center on the maturity of believers. Some leaders reveal their lack of a pastor-teacher's heart by what concerns them. If the main focus of your ministry is planting churches, then maybe you're an apostle; if your primary concern is winning people to Christ, then maybe you're an evangelist; if your great love and desire is preaching and proclaiming God's Word to multitudes, then maybe you're the prophet; and if you love to work with a group of people you call your flock and watch them grow to maturity and begin to minister to one another, then maybe you're a pastor-teacher.

Leadership in God's church is based on ability. But it is ability that God gives. Gifts are the result of grace. We do nothing to deserve them or earn them. Christ gave these gifted leaders to the church and equips them with His authority and ability to minister to others. It is important to discover if you are one of these four leaders. It will immediately tell you the kind of ministry you should develop. It will give direction to your life and relieve you of much frustration in trying to be something or someone you are not.

Leader's Checklist

1. Do you believe that God has chosen you as a leader for His church? Write down some reasons why you feel this way.

2. Do you have the desire of the apostle, to build churches and train leaders to take over when you leave?

3. Do you believe God has called you to preach?

4. Are you an effective public speaker? How can you tell?

5. Do you enjoy talking to people about Christ? How do they usually respond?

6. Would you rather share your faith in Christ with nonbelievers, than spend most of your time building up other believers?

7. Do you desire to minister to a group of believers you can call your own?

8. Do you tend to concentrate on the maturity of believers, rather than the salvation of nonbelievers?

9. Do you love to teach God's Word and study for that ministry?

DO SPIRITUAL GIFTS HELP?

Among the many spiritual gifts listed in the New Testament are two gifts that refer to leadership. One we shall call the gift of leadership (see Rom. 12:8), which is also translated "ruling," or "managing." The other we shall call the gift of administration (see 1 Cor. 12:28), which is also called "governments."

For many years now I have noticed enormous differences in the leadership styles of people in the ministry. I have tried to look for common ingredients that will help us build leaders for the future. Often I ran into a dead-end street! There were some basic things that I discovered that kept coming to my attention, however. I wasn't always sure why these things existed, but they were there. Let me explain what I'm talking about!

• Some leaders were motivators; some were organizers.
• Some worked best in front of people; others at a desk.
• Some ad-libbed much of the time; others needed a chart or job description.
• Some demanded specific goals; others liked to solve present problems.

- Some cared little about costs; others always had dollar signs before them.
- Some derived authority from others; others had authority in themselves.
- Some organized around people; others organized around jobs and tasks.
- Some were excitable; others were stable and calm.
- Some were filled with new ideas; others spent time evaluating ideas.
- Some kept no schedules; others were very disciplined.
- Some had cluttered desks; others were spotless.
- Some were fun people to be around; others were dry, dull, and boring.
- Some loved to talk; others said very little.

The list could go on and on. There were tremendous differences in people. Yet, each was a leader. Styles were different, but all produced results.

What can we learn from all this? Differences do exist. Don't be too critical of another's leadership. Perhaps if we study the passages that describe the gift of leadership we will have a better understanding of the different styles of leadership.

Do You Have the Gift of Leadership?—Romans 12:8

Romans 12:8 identifies leadership as: "He who leads, with diligence." The word "leads" is based on two words, "to stand" and "before." To stand before people is the root idea of this gift of leadership. It refers to a person who motivates others and sees leadership primarily as it relates to people, not tasks. It is used eight times in the New Testament, as well as several times in the Greek Old Testament.

In the New Testament, it refers to fathers (see 1 Tim. 3:4,12), bishops (see 1 Tim. 3:5), deacons (see 1 Tim. 3:12), elders (see 1 Tim. 5:17), and believers who meet needs and do good works (see Titus 3:8,14). It was used in Greek literature before Christ in the sense of presiding or conducting meetings. Another idea was that of protector. Out of this came meanings of assisting, helping, and caring for others. Let's consider some of the facts about this gift.

It is a qualification of elders (bishops) and deacons which is based on their home life (see 1 Tim. 3:4,5,12). It refers to the way a man handles his children. He leads them by keeping them under control with all dignity. Dignity points to a seriousness of purpose and self-respect. One's children should reflect their understanding of the position of their father. The father should reflect a seriousness about his family, considering their needs of discipline, teaching, and proper motivation. They should look up to his leadership.

It is to be done with diligence (see Rom. 12:8). The description of this spiritual gift includes a simple phrase that is given in order to help us identify the kind of leadership that is given by the Holy Spirit. The words "with diligence" refer to "haste" or "speed." The one who has this gift is noted for the speed with which he responds to needs that exist. Those who take their time about responding are evidencing that the spiritual gift is not there or that they are not being obedient to the promptings of the Spirit of God.

It is a desire to meet needs (see Titus 3:8,14). In contrast to those who see leadership as one who gives orders to other people, the Bible teaches that the one with this gift is one who desires to meet needs. In order to accomplish this (according to Titus 3), one must involve himself in what Titus calls "good deeds." This fits with our Lord's constant instruction that those who would be greatest and in positions of authority must learn to serve others. It is interesting to see how important Paul believed good deeds are. In Titus 2:7, Paul says, "In all things show yourself to be an example of good deeds." Then in Titus 2:14, he says that one of the purposes of redemption is to have a people who are "zealous for good deeds." Titus 3:1 states that we are "to be ready for every good deed." And, of course, the admonition in Titus 3:8 and 14 connects "good deeds" with our word for "leadership," and emphasizes that these good deeds will meet pressing needs in the lives of those for whom the leader is responsible.

It involves taking care of people (see 1 Tim. 3:5). This passage puts the word for leadership in parallel structure with the words "take care of." Leadership means taking care of people. The words "take care of" involve the direction of the mind toward the object cared for. It suggests loving interest and certainly the idea of protection. A good illustration of this would be the story of the Good Samaritan in Luke 10. In verses 34 and 35 of that chapter this same word of 1 Timothy 3:5 is used and translated to "take care of." When the Good Samaritan finished caring for the injured man's wounds, he brought him to the inn and, according to verse 35, he provided some money for the innkeeper and said, "Take care of him," and then promised to pay any additional expenses. This illustration of "taking care of" people involves the matter of material or financial provision. Those with the gift of spiritual leadership would obviously be caring for the spiritual needs of the people under their leadership. (Note: It seems like it would apply also to material and physical needs as well.)

A man's responsibility to take care of his family involves providing for their needs, protecting them from dangers along the way, and maintaining discipline and control as the leader of the home. A spiritual leader must also take care of those for whom he is responsible.

There must be a proper sense of authority and chain of command, but it appears that the response factor to his leadership is based upon the qualities of his home life as well as his loving concern for those around him. He is a protector of people who understands that "love covers a multitude of sins." He cares for the personal needs of those he leads, seeking their good at all times. He is known by his "good deeds" in seeking to meet the needs in people's lives. While all those in positions of leadership should seek to emulate these principles, some are uniquely gifted by God. It is not by training, education, or natural talent that these lead, but because of God's grace and the unique ministry of the Holy Spirit. What a joy it is to work with those in whom we see the Spirit-controlled life and temperament, as well as those who are gifted by the Holy Spirit for that ministry of leadership.

The person with the gift of leadership will usually be a motivator of others. He works out of a desire to see people grow and develop. He will lead in order to meet needs. When a need exists, he responds quickly. He loves to set goals for other people and to work by them himself. He has a sense of accomplishment when goals are completed. He organizes primarily through people. He spends most of his time in leadership talking with people, helping them to see their problems and how they can be more effective.

One of our staff members who fits this picture came to my office to discuss his ministry. Our entire conversation dealt with the goals he had for himself and others. It was amusing as well as thrilling. God made him like that and he is doing a tremendous job. He sees his worth and value through the goals he has set. As long as his goals are based on biblical and spiritual objectives, God will bless his leadership.

Do You Have the Gift of Administration?
—1 Corinthians 12:28

The very sound of the word "administration" frightens many people! Administration is the dirty word that is necessary in every organization. It is a thankless job that rarely is appreciated by others. But, it has to be done! Those who do administration without a gift in that area can be quickly spotted. They are frustrated with details and complain about having too much to do. They procrastinate. Things pile up on them. There never seems to be enough time to get things done. They are uptight with people. They worry. They're overwhelmed with the responsibility they have. They need a break (so does everyone else!).

The word "administration" in 1 Corinthians 12:28 is used three times in the New Testament and several times in the Greek Old Testament. It means to "steer a ship." It refers to the pilot or helmsman. The word "guide" was often used to describe the work of this person in ancient times.

Proverbs 12:5 uses this same Greek word in reference to the wicked when it says, "The thoughts of the righteous are just, but the *counsels* of the wicked are deceitful." It carries the idea of counsel in the book of Proverbs, especially as it relates to guidance or direction. It is used in the writings of Plato to refer to one who knows the times of the day and the year, the sky, the stars, currents of air, etc. This knowledge was, of course, beneficial to keeping a ship on course. Our modern idea of "navigator" would fit this usage. In gathering the evidence behind the usage of this word, we can learn several things:

It refers to one responsible for the direction of things. The "helmsman" was responsible to steer the ship, but he is not the same as the owner of the ship. This is obvious from a passage like Acts 27:11. Sometimes we confuse the responsibility and accountability of one who owns the ship with the one who has been employed to run the affairs of the ship in terms of getting it to its proper destination. If the ship is to be applied to the local church as it was frequently done by early church history, then the owner would be the Lord, and the "helmsman" could refer to those responsible for the direction of the church. The "helmsman" must navigate the ship on a proper course. He keeps the ship from losing its way or from various dangers along the way. One who has this gift would be characterized by the ability to make decisions that affect the direction in which the "ship" (or church) should go, and that, obviously, should be the direction in which the Word of God teaches it should go! The person with this gift is concerned about keeping the church (or any group within it) on course with what the Word of God says it should be doing.

It refers to one who makes decisions. We have all heard the phrase "the buck stops here." The point is that at some person's desk the chain of command must stop, and a final decision made. When the safety of the cargo and passengers is at stake, one must be able to make decisions that will guarantee the safe arrival of the ship to its proper destination. The goal for believers is maturity (see Col. 1:28), and those with this gift would be concerned about any methods or practices that would detract from that goal. They would concentrate on that which reaches the goal. Decisions must be made. Sometimes that means "cutting back" certain methods, practices, personnel, financial support, etc., in order to keep the "ship" on a safe course! The ability to make decisions is an important function of this gift. While every one of us must make decisions from time to time, not all

74

of us have that God-given ability to make decisions in behalf of many others. There is much risk involved, and the danger of failure is constantly in front of you. But, those with the gift have the God-given courage and ability to make those decisions.

It is based upon one's character and conduct. Proverbs 12:5 points out that the counsels (our word) of the wicked are deceitful. It is a godly life-style that makes the decisions of the "helmsman" what they should be. Ezekiel 27 in its context clearly shows that principle also. Sinful practices will diminish our ability to make correct decisions in terms of spiritual leadership.

It suggests one who has a strong sense of responsibility and accountability. We can certainly see that in terms of a ship's cargo and passengers. How tragic it would be to have a person making decisions that affect the lives of many people without any sense of responsibility toward those people! But the real issue here in terms of accountability is that the "helmsman" does not own the ship, but is employed by the owner of the ship and fully accountable to the owner for the safe arrival of the cargo and passengers. The "owner" in spiritual matters is the Lord Himself. This point is clearly emphasized in Hebrews 13:17 when it says: "Obey your leaders, and submit to them; for they keep watch over your souls, as *those who will give an account.* Let them do this with joy and not with grief, for this would be unprofitable for you" (italics added).

The One to whom we must give account is the Lord Himself. Romans 14:12 says, "So then each one of us shall give account of himself to God." Leaders are answerable to God for the decisions they make and the direction they give.

It is greatly needed in time of storm. When things are running "smoothly" no one seems to notice the presence of the "helmsman," nor do they sense their need of his direction and leadership. But when the waves of life come pouring over the sides of our ship, and the storm increases in intensity, then everyone must out of necessity look to the "helmsman" for leadership. The test of one with the gift of administration is the ability to "weather the storm" and to steer the ship back on course. There are many "storms" along the way in the work of God. Churches and Christian organizations often seem to be sinking, or at least they seem to be tossed around by the waves of difficulty and trials. At a time like that, spiritual leaders with the gift of administration are greatly needed. They bring calm into the hearts of those in the storm, and decisions are made which will bring the "ship" safely through the storm.

Those with the gift of administration sense accountability for what happens. Those with the gift of leadership make things happen. The administrator can put it on paper much easier than the gifted leader can. The leadership type would rather talk with people. The administrator needs time alone away from people. He must think carefully about the decisions that are to be made. The one with the gift of leadership responds immediately to a need, while the administrator needs time to think about its ramifications and effects on others. The leadership person wonders why we can't do it now; the administrator knows why.

These two gifts make a great team! Two are better than one, provided that they understand each other's gifts and allow each other the freedom to exercise those gifts. What is missing in the administrator is found in the gift of leadership, and vice versa. They need each other.

It was my joy to experience the struggles of leadership and administration with a dear friend in the ministry. He and I worked together for seven years. He now has a great and growing ministry on his own. We learned much about each other and the differences between us. Time and maturity have shown us many similarities. We are both leaders. We both love to teach and preach. He is a better motivator than I with people, and I learned so many things from him. I hope he learned from me. I think in some ways, I am a better administrator. We are still good friends (in case you wondered!). We both struggled with the study of spiritual gifts, and saw how very important it was to our relationships with each other.

Some are gifted and some are not. Often we must do what we do even though we are not gifted in that area. We exercise a role in that situation. There is a sense in which all of us can exercise leadership, trusting God to help us. If we have the spiritual gift of leadership, our task is easier. Regardless, we can all learn the principles of these gifts and profit by them, with God's strength.

Leader's Checklist

1. Do you like to work with people more than with specific tasks? What are some clues that tell you which you prefer?

2. Do you desire to meet needs immediately when you see them?

3. Do you sense a desire to take care of people under your leadership?

4. Do you feel responsible for things? How many things? Do you have to "do it all"?

5. Can you make decisions quickly in times of stress and difficulty?

6. Are you willing to take risks in order to grow as a person? Can you name three recent instances in which you took risks?

PART IV

MOTIVATION: WHY DO YOU WANT TO BE A LEADER?

7
BE CAREFUL
ABOUT YOURSELF

Why do we do what we do? Jeremiah 17:9,10 seems to indicate that we cannot know ourselves; that we are deceitful and wicked. Only God knows what we are really like. That's why we need to study His manual (Bible). He reveals much about our motivations.

The business world is concerned about motivation because the corporate profits are involved. Views today of success and failure are often related to motivation. The so-called "goodies" of life (Christians call these "blessings") are seemingly reserved for those who are highly motivated.

The advertising industry is concerned with motivation. They tell us frequently why what we are wearing is no good anymore. They remind us that the "things" we have are getting old and in sad need of repair. We are being motivated to buy a new product, of course.

Psychologists have long been aware of the importance of motivation. Behavior patterns, whether good or bad, can be directly traced to the motivations people have. Decisions, major or minor, are affected by motivations.

Much time is spent in introspection and analysis of why a person reacts the way he does.

In leadership, motivation is vital to people's response. People quickly question the wisdom of a leader's decision today because they have been affected by leaders with wrong motives yesterday. We hear such things as "He's in it for himself," or "I'm going to get what's coming to me," or "They're all alike; you can't trust them!" When someone appears to be successful, people will say, "If you really knew him, you would know why he's doing that!" We question people's motives.

There are six areas in which the spiritual leader must be careful about himself. Each one of these represents improper motivation that can destroy the effectiveness of the spiritual leader.

Be Careful About Position Which Leads to Pride

The desire of one who wants to be first in everything is rooted in pride (which the Lord hates). It is concerned about lofty titles and fancy offices. It covets public recognition and seeks to parade itself before the eyes of others. A person motivated by position is inclined more to emphasize his authority than his service to others.

Position blinds your eyes to the feelings of those around or under you. Decisions are made without understanding and compassion. Authority is viewed as a title or job description (which, of course, is a part of it), rather than a responsibility that only God can make possible.

In saying all of this, we do not mean that titles, offices, and job descriptions are unimportant or should be disregarded. God has a chain of command in the home, church, government, business, etc. We are instructed to be submissive to all kinds of authority, regardless of the motivations or spiritual caliber of those in authority. It is the attitude of the leader that is our concern, not the responsibility of those under that leadership.

Jesus illustrated this problem in His remarks about the scribes and Pharisees (see Matt. 23:6-12). Their problem was the desire for honor and position. They loved the "place of honor" and the "chief seats in the synagogues." They wanted to be treated with respect. They knew little of what it is to be a servant.

Three basic reasons explain a leader's desire for position.

He wants to be the ultimate authority. It's hard for people motivated by position to be subservient to others. On every decision and plan they desire to be the final answer. There is a time when those in authority must make the final decision, but any leader with experience and much responsibility will quickly tell you what a burden such authority can be upon your life. Your decisions affect the lives of other people. The best leader has a servant's heart. He shows no partiality, but learns to be "slave to all" (see Mark 10:42-45).

He wants to dominate others. This feeling can arise out of a poor and insecure self-image. If a person is insecure in himself or in his job he will tend to dominate others. It gives him a measure of satisfaction to know that he can do this with others. It arises out of pride, not humility. It fails to recognize the importance of each individual. It refuses to accept differences of opinion. Sometimes it results for such a leader because he fears failure. He tries to hide his own mistakes and inadequacies before others by dominating and controlling.

He wants people to respect him and look up to him. High position makes people take notice, or so he thinks! The leader motivated by position feels that the "best seats" and the "better service" goes to the people of great position. The desire to have others respect you is a reflection on your self-esteem. Respect is the result of a godly life-style and consistent character, not high position. If your life-style is not pleasing to the Lord, people can outwardly appear respectful, but inwardly resent your leadership.

I knew a man once who was controlled by the desire for high position. It was manifested in the way he talked, walked, and dressed. People who worked for him said he was proud and domineering. A visit to his office revealed his problem. All kinds of awards, plaques, trophies and letters of commendation cluttered his office. They seemed like "security blankets." I felt sorry for him. He was lonely and unhappy. Very insecure.

What's the solution to this problem of leadership to which we all are tempted? Humility; evaluating yourself in the light of God's approval and commendation; being a servant to all. That's the only solution. Away with all the props that are artificial and superficial, the little crutches we lean on to prove how important we are. Be done with lesser things. Graduate up to the role of servant. That's the place of greatest joy!

Be Careful About Money Being Your Motivation

Leaders need to be very careful about themselves in the area of money. Motivations in the secular world are controlled by the dollar sign. Money is not sinful in itself, but loving it is (see 1 Tim. 6:10). You are not spiritual because you are poor. Money is simply a tool, not a master to control you (see Matt. 6:24). Money-love or the desire to get rich can cause many other problems (see 1 Tim. 6:9,10).

A friend of mine left the ministry because of bad debts. He was not careful and it cost him his leadership. Another friend left the ministry because money became more important to him than ministry. He enjoyed being rich and the pleasures money could afford. He also lost his leadership.

Why does money cause such problems? Why do leaders forfeit the blessing of God upon their ministry because of a few shekels? How does money affect the exercise of spiritual leadership? Ask yourself these three questions:

Do I exercise my leadership because I am paid? When your reason for doing what you do is because you are paid for it or because it is a requirement that affects your salary, then your leadership is weakened. Some pastors evaluate the Lord's will in leading them to a church on the basis of the salary they will be paid. It is best to make such a decision without knowing what the salary will be. If it is more than you make now, you might want the job for the wrong reason; if it is less than you make now, you might reject it for the wrong reason.

Several years ago I was traveling to a meeting without a great deal of money in my pocket. In fact, I wasn't sure I could return without getting some gas for my car. On the way there I began thinking about the honorarium I might receive even though none was promised. I thought about how much it should be, and what my reactions would be upon receiving it. I wondered if I should ask for it in cash so I could get the gas I needed to get home. Well, I decided to keep quiet about it. I stood around after the meeting waiting for some assurance about the honorarium, but none was given. As I got in my car to drive home, I found a root of bitterness growing. I soon realized that my motive was completely wrong in speaking at that occasion. I was doing it because of the possibility of being paid. Well, the Lord didn't let me off the hook on that one! I never did get an honorarium! (By the way, the gas miraculously lasted until I got home!)

Churches and Christian organizations should take care of the financial arrangements of guests who minister to them as surely as the leaders who are daily ministering to them. Leaders should not be muzzled or hindered in their work by the lack of financial support. But on the other hand, leaders should not do what they do because of the money they might receive. We must do it as unto the Lord. He alone must control our motivations.

Do you exercise your leadership because you need the money? Some people don't get motivated at all unless they need the money. It seems more and more difficult to get people to respond without paying them. In many cases, we ought to pay people for what they do, but on the other hand, there are many situations in which pay is not justified. It can rob the individual of serving voluntarily. If you do something because you need the money and it is not the payment you expected or wanted, you will soon discover a spirit of resentment or personal hurt.

Do you exercise your leadership because you want to get rich? Many leaders today are doing what they are doing because of a desire for financial gain. Money is the number one motivation. Paul warned us about this problem in 1 Timothy 6:9,10. It is hard to respect a person as a spiritual leader, much less respond to them, when you know this is the motivation.

What's the answer to the problem of money? How does a leader avoid the wrong motivations? One word answers—contentment. Paul wrote of this quality in Philippians 4:11-13 and spoke of what he had learned. God has promised to supply our needs. We need to trust Him. Paul, in 1 Timothy 6:7, tells us that we brought nothing into this world and we will take nothing out of it. Godliness with contentment is great gain. Contentment is based on inward trust in a faithful God who has promised to supply all your need (see Phil. 4:19).

Be Careful About Wanting to Be Famous

Fame is in the heart of the leader who is impressed by his own achievements. The leader troubled by this problem loves to read his "press clippings." He's concerned with proper introductions and resumes with long lists of honors. He evaluates his effectiveness by who knows about him.

One day certain Jewish leaders sent priests and Levites from Jerusalem to meet John the Baptist in the wilderness. They wanted to know who he thought he was. John told them, "I am a voice of one crying in the wilderness" (John 1:23). He said his ministry was to prepare the way of the Lord. He didn't feel worthy to untie the thong of the Lord's sandal. He remarked in John 3:30: "He must increase, but I must decrease."

Paul wrote in Galatians 6:14, "But may it never be that I should boast except in the cross of our Lord Jesus Christ, through which the world has been crucified to me, and I to the world."

Some want fame because they desire people to know how great they are. Others want it because they want to be like someone else. Some feel it makes them important. Proverbs 27:2 says, "Let another praise you, and not your own mouth; a stranger, and not your own lips." Our one desire should be the glory of God Himself. In 1 Corinthians 1:29 Paul says, "That no man should boast before God," and in verse 31 of the same chapter, "Let him who boasts, boast in the Lord."

A person whose life is controlled by wanting to be famous needs self-denial. By self-denial we don't mean asceticism or false humility, but the desire to give all the glory to God. It is a willingness to be unnoticed so that

Jesus is recognized by all. It is putting aside selfish ambition, submitting yourself to the Lord of all who alone is worthy of praise! Practicing self-denial is a commitment to praise and thank God for everything. To Him be all the glory!

Be Careful About Personal Needs

The fourth area of problems facing the leader is that of personal needs. It is good to be motivated by the needs of others, but it is dangerous for the leader to be motivated by his own needs.

We need encouragement. We all need it. Leadership is lonely. Sometimes your need for encouragement is greater than you can bear, so you do what you do in order to have people encourage you. Watch out! The Lord knows your needs before you ask Him. We are to bear the burdens of others (see Gal. 6:2), and learn to bear our own (see Gal. 6:5).

Self-pity can set in on the leader who becomes exhausted in the exercise of his leadership. The result can be laziness, apathy, and indifference. Sometimes we need a "kick in the pants," rather than the sympathy of others!

The only solution is to trust God to meet your needs. The Lord is "the God of all comfort," and He understands better than anyone else. Take your burdens to the Lord and leave them there! Cast all your anxiety upon Him, He cares for you (see 1 Pet. 5:7).

We need physical affection. Everybody likes strokes (physical affection)! A warm handshake, an arm around the shoulder, a brief embrace, a pat on the back are simple but effective ways to say "I love you" or "I appreciate you."

But, it's dangerous to exercise leadership when you have a need for physical affection. Leaders seem vulnerable in this area. It's almost a paradox: strong leaders seem above such a need, yet all leaders know how lonely they can become and how welcome is a show of affection.

Ecclesiastes 3 reminds us that there is a time for everything. Often the problem is one of timing. Leaders must guard against bad timing in showing physical affection. A few suggestions:

(1) Don't give physical affection out of a sexual need, unless to your marital partner. When you feel aroused in a situation or attracted by the opposite sex, it is dangerous to show physical affection. A friend of mine was counseling with a lady in his office who was quite attractive. She was having marriage problems and was near an emotional breakdown. With many tears she embraced my friend for a moment of comfort. In that moment, they both felt a strong attraction toward one another. One thing led to another, and after several weeks of continual counseling and contact, they went too far. Both lives were damaged. When evaluating the situation much later after repentance and restoration, my friend realized that at the time he had a sexual need. He and his wife were not ministering to one another as the Bible teaches. His desires got the best of him.

(2) Don't give physical affection to members of the opposite sex when you are alone or isolated from other people. This is only common sense, but the testimony of many leaders supports the wisdom of repeating it. Jesus told us (Matt. 26:41), "The spirit is willing, but the flesh is weak." Don't trust your ability to control your desires! Trust God and do all you can to prevent trouble before it happens.

The answer to the problem of personal needs in the heart of the leader is trust in the Lord. There is no substitution! "The Lord is my shepherd, I shall not want" (Ps. 23:1). He has promised to meet our needs. Trust Him to do it!

Be Careful About Feeling Obligated

Duty can be a good thing, but it can also lead to improper motivations. Some leaders feel obligated to lead; they are unhappy and weary with the responsibility of leadership; there is a lack of joy and enthusiasm. This leader does what he does because he thinks if he didn't, people would not like him as much. He feels an obligation to perform in order to have people respond to him. On the other side of the coin, the leader sometimes feels that if he doesn't do what is expected of him, people will consider him to be a failure. The fear of failure drives many a leader!

Another problem is that of guilt. Leaders feel guilty if they do not do what is expected of them. Therefore, they work harder out of obligation than before. Guilt drives them.

The obligation many feel in being a leader arises out of a bad self-image. A lack of self-worth is behind it. Often, this leader has not learned to accept himself in the light of God's love and forgiveness. The leader fails to rest in the Lord. He is pressuring himself to perform.

The only answer is the joy of the Holy Spirit; leading because you are thrilled with the opportunity! Joy goes out the window when we do not relax in the love of God and enjoy the people around us. There is little joy when we impose standards upon ourselves that no one else put there. God loves you, leader! He can fill your heart with joy in exercising your leadership. You have value because of God—it's as simple as that!

Beware the "Success Syndrome"

This leader must meet his goals. They are the chief

motivating force in his life. Goals are good, but they become improper when controlled by the "more syndrome." We want "more than last year." This person must do better than the previous year or he senses failure.

The desire to achieve can be good and productive, but it can also detract and hinder us in accomplishing the will of God. Some leaders are pressured by "success-oriented" people. They have charts and diagrams to prove their point (and often their value). Behind this is the matter of comparison. Some leaders spend all their free moments comparing themselves with other leaders, trying to prove to themselves that they are doing better or more than others. Numbers play an important part to the leader motivated by achievement. Numbers become the test of "success." If more people were involved this week over last, this month over last, or this year over last, then we are successful.

What's the answer to this problem? Peace, resting in the sovereignty of God, not apathy and indifference. Evaluating yourself with others is not the answer. Resting in the Lord is. His "well done" is given on the basis of faithfulness. He judges us for what we have done for Him, not in comparison to another's gifts, talents, or achievements.

Summary

In summary let us review the problems leaders may encounter and what the Bible teaches are the solutions.

The problem of *position*, which can lead to pride, is solved by *humility*. Mark 10:37,40-45 illustrates Jesus' answer to the person who wants position: James and John said to Him, "Grant that we may sit in Your glory, one on Your right, and one on Your left."

" 'To sit on My right or on My left, this is not Mine

to give; but it is for those for whom it has been prepared.'

"And hearing this, the ten began to feel indignant toward James and John. And calling them to Himself, Jesus said to them, 'You know that those who are recognized as rulers of the Gentiles lord it over them; and their great men exercise authority over them. But it is not so among you, but whoever wishes to become great among you shall be your servant; and whoever wishes to be first among you shall be slave of all. For even the Son of Man did not come to be served, but to serve, and to give His life a ransom for many.'"

To the problem of the love of *money*, Paul said that the solution was *contentment*: "Not that I speak from want; for I have learned to be content in whatever circumstances I am. I know how to get along with humble means, and I also know how to live in prosperity; in any and every circumstance I have learned the secret of being filled and going hungry, both of having abundance and suffering need. I can do all things through Him who strengthens me .... And my God shall supply all your needs according to His riches in glory in Christ Jesus" (Phil. 4:11-13,19).

The solution to the problem of wanting *fame* is to learn *self-denial.* Paul, in 1 Corinthians 1:29,31, says, "No man should boast before God .... Let him who boasts, boast in the Lord." John the Baptist said of Christ, "He must increase, but I must decrease" (John 3:30).

The concern for *personal needs* can be solved by *trusting* in God. Peter says to cast "all your anxiety upon Him, because He cares for you" (1 Pet. 5:7). David in Psalm 23 says "the Lord is my shepherd, I shall not want."

The leader who leads out of feeling *obligated* to serve lacks *joy* and enthusiasm. Paul says, in Romans 14:17,

"For the kingdom of God is . . . righteousness and peace and joy in the Holy Spirit."

Finally, the leader who finds his motivation in *achieving*, is evaluating himself with others. He needs to rest in the Lord, to find *peace*. "Thou wilt keep him in perfect peace, whose mind is stayed on thee: because he trusteth in thee" (Isa. 26:3, *KJV*).

Leader's Checklist

1. Have you ever desired a higher position to feel important? Describe the situation.

2. On a scale of 1-10 rate yourself on why you work as a leader.

1	2	3	4	5	6	7	8	9	10
For what I receive								For what I can give	

3. Do you want to get rich?

4. Do you refrain from drawing praise from others, but rather redirect it toward the Lord?

5. Do you have personal needs that you are failing to trust God for? List these.

6. Do you sense that you do what you do out of obligation rather than joy? What can you do about this?

7. Do you spend a good deal of time comparing yourself with others? To whom do you compare yourself? Why?

8. Do you do what you do because you feel guilty if you don't? Name some instances.

9. Do numbers affect your leadership? Do you get discouraged easily when the numbers are less? Do large numbers make you proud?

DOING THINGS FOR THE RIGHT REASONS

What makes a leader resort to wrong motives like those discussed in the previous chapter? Sin, of course, will do it every time! But, what other matters make a leader susceptible? How can a leader be sure he is doing things for the right reasons?

In the early years of my ministry as a leader I did not understand these things as clearly as I see them now. It almost takes experience itself to show you how these things can affect your leadership. I have always wanted to do God's will and to live for His glory, but sometimes I get in the way. I don't mean to, it just comes naturally! The following seven problems have greatly affected my leadership at one time or another. Excuse me for being so personal, but I didn't know any other way to share with you what I believe is important for all leaders to understand.

Why Does a Leader Have Wrong Motivations?

When results are few and far between a leader gets discouraged. You will often doubt and question your leadership when that happens. However, before you get completely depressed and write that letter of resignation (usually on Monday mornings!), you'd better keep a few things in mind.

First of all, you may have the wrong set of results in your mind and heart. You may be set more on numbers and charts than on individual people who are being built up and encouraged by your leadership. God told Isaiah (see Isa. 6) to go and tell people His message but He said they would not respond. Most of us would have quit right there and then! Isaiah's responsibility was to be faithful to God, regardless of the results.

Secondly, the problem may be a lack of faith and vision on your part, and that is why you see so few results. Don't blame the people, you're the leader! What do you believe God can do in your situation? Without faith, you can't please the Lord (see Heb. 11:6). God honors our faith. He is sovereign in what He does, but I have discovered that He coincides His sovereignty with my faith in Him so that my joy is made full!

Thirdly, you may not be working hard enough. Some of us don't seem to enjoy work. Maybe you are lazy and indifferent, and that is why you see such few results. You need to get right with God and get to work! God puts no premium on laziness or apathy.

A staff member in our church was ready to give up due to a lack of results in his ministry. I tried to sympathize and encourage him, but it didn't seem to help. Then, one of the secretaries told me how lazy he was and that the work was piling up. He was not following through on contacts that were given him, nor answering his telephone calls. He spent many hours at his desk just thinking (a necessary thing at times, but it can be overdone). After putting the facts together, I called him into my office, and this time the conversation was not one of sympathy and encouragement! It was get to work or get another job! It was amazing to me how quickly his attitude changed as well as the results in his ministry!

Some leaders don't handle criticism from others very well. Some get mad, and some cry. Some get ulcers, and some seek revenge by using their leadership to hurt or hinder those criticizing.

The only way I know to avoid criticism is to say nothing, do nothing, and be nothing (printed on a plaque in my office). But saying that, still doesn't mean I like to be criticized. Who does? My problem is the same as yours—learning how to handle criticism when it comes, and in my case, it's a weekly problem.

First, realize the possibility that you may deserve it. I know this hurts to admit, but sometimes leaders deserve the criticism they are receiving. Maybe what people are saying is the truth! Can you face it? Can you learn from it?

Second, you may create that kind of environment. If you are a critical person, you can expect to receive much of it in return. The older I get the more aware I am of the damaging effects of criticism that is not biblical and constructive. I don't want to listen to it, yet there's something about my old sin nature that wants to be critical of others and to hear criticism about other people. Lord, deliver us! I try to avoid hearing what critical people have to say. I don't want to be around them. If I can't say something nice about a person, why say anything at all? I realize that at times criticism may be justified and right, but much of what I have seen that people call "constructive criticism" is questionable. Be careful what you say concerning others. Learn to compliment them and look for the positive qualities in their lives.

When someone shares a critical remark about another person with you, learn to answer with a positive statement concerning that person. Find something commendable in that person's life and draw attention to it. Your leadership will grow.

Third, remember that criticism is intended to make us stronger as leaders, not weaker. When criticism comes your way that you know is not justified, learn to accept it and be thankful for it, knowing that God will use the experience to make you stronger. It will help you to reflect more of His love toward others. Many times we learn what not to do by the things people say about us. That's worth something, you know!

No one can expect a leader to be free from criticism. The very fact that you are a leader opens the door for others to criticize you. You are out front, easy to spot, and easy to blame. When someone says a critical remark to you, just say "thank you" to that person. Sometimes you can say, "Thanks for telling me about that; I'm sure the Lord had a reason behind the fact that you told me." Another positive way to respond is, "Thank you for caring enough about me to criticize me." Or, you can say, "Please pray for me that I will learn to do things as God wants me to do."

Sometimes a leader gets little cooperation. This can eat the heart out of you if you don't watch it! You begin to question your leadership because others are not cooperating. But before your motivations get all confused, ask yourself two questions. The first one is, "Do the people know what to do?" If they don't, how can you expect them to cooperate? It's really not their fault. A lack of communication or information on what to do can produce this condition.

We planned to have a tremendous outreach program one fall, but we started too late and failed to communicate properly to the people. It was no surprise that very few people showed up for this great adventure!

The second question is, "Are you leading the way in this matter?" If you are asking them to do something that you will not do, then it is no surprise that there is little cooperation.

Another important thing to rely upon when there is little cooperation is the fact that you and God make a majority! Leaders need to stand alone at times. Some people are waiting to cooperate in order to first see what you are like.

Loneliness is the price of leadership. Very few people (leaders are an exception) will understand what it's like to be a leader. They will not know what you are going through, and they will not know how to help. That friend you need is hard to find. Of course, the Lord is with you, so you are never really alone (see Matt. 28:20; Heb. 13:5). Here are a few suggestions that I have found helpful in meeting the problem of loneliness.

There are different levels and kinds of friendship. You do not have to receive everything you need from one person. Some people will be social friends that are fun to have dinner with or with whom you can enjoy a bit of recreation. Others are great for just talking by the fireplace or over a cup of coffee. You need people who can listen well without being critical. Some friends are great in a crisis, they seem like family. You can call on them for an emergency. There are a few in leadership positions who do understand and under proper conditions you will find close friendships with them. One caution about close friendships with other leaders: Make sure there is no competition between you, and that you do not constantly compare yourself with the other leader or his ministry.

The major hurdle to get over is trying to do everything with one person or another couple. It usually doesn't work that way. Learn to enjoy friendships with many people and don't have too many expectations about what you will receive from them. If you enjoy a friendship with someone by participating in athletic competition, don't assume that your marital partners will be good friends also. My wife may enjoy shopping with a particular lady, but it doesn't mean that that lady's husband and I will be close friends.

It has been my observation that close and intimate friendships take a long time to develop. Be patient and don't try to be close right away. There is a time for building confidence between you and your friend. Most friendships we have are really acquaintances or based on social occasions. The circle of friends in this category can be great. Enjoy them all! There are close friendships in life that are built on serious communication or a time of deep need or crisis. There is something "special" about those friends that were there to help when you needed it. The circle of friends like this is much smaller. Intimate friends with whom you can share anything without fear of being rejected or criticized compose a very small circle. Some people have only one other intimate friend besides their marital partner in their entire life. Five to ten people would probably be the maximum for most of us in our lifetimes.

When I sense deep loneliness, for whatever reason, I must remember first that the Lord is with me and to share my feelings with Him. Secondly, I turn to those intimate friends with whom I can freely talk. My wife is my best friend in that regard! In addition to my wife, I have found my best friends to be those with whom I have worked in our church.

Before you let self-pity and discouragement grip you in a time of loneliness, ask yourself if *you* are seeking to be a friend to anyone. It is more important to be a friend than to have one. In fact, it seems like when you seek to be a friend to others, God rewards you with friends who will minister to you.

Having said all of that, I must still remind every leader and leader-to-be, that loneliness is a price to pay in being a spiritual leader. The higher you are in the levels of any organization, the more loneliness you will sense. Learn to accept it and to trust God to meet your need.

Sometimes a heavy work load seems too great to bear! The danger here is that you start doing things to solve this problem that are unwise or based on hasty decisions. The next day or the next week may be a different situation. You'll feel differently about a heavy work load after a few days pass. But what if you don't? Suppose you are continually swamped, and there is no letting up. What do you do?

One of the first things you should do is to ask for an assistant, someone to help alleviate the heavy work load. It might be a secretary or another leader who can take over some of your responsibilities. But, before you make that decision, consider some of the reasons why you are experiencing the heavy work load: (1) You are incompetent (ouch!) to meet the demands of the job; (2) No one is competent to meet the demands of the job! (That's better!); (3) No staff or lay job descriptions: There is constant overlap and neglect so that the job usually falls back on your desk; (4) You can't trust others to do what you are doing; (5) You take on too much work that no one told you to do (you're probably a "workaholic"); (6) Your priorities are all messed up; (7) You are physically tired or emotionally exhausted; (8) You like people to think you are busy and overworked; (9) You're nervous and keyed up most of the time—you must work; (10) You think the organization depends so much upon you that if you don't keep at it, everything will fall apart!

Enough of the problems. What about some solutions? Let's start with some practical suggestions for yourself. Make a list of things you want to accomplish each day and check them off when completed. Some leaders do that the first thing in the morning; others do it the night before so they can sleep better! Don't procrastinate! If you can do it today, then do it. Don't put something off until tomorrow that you could really do today. Strive for a clean desk every day.

Determine what things you presently do that could be done by others. Evaluate those things that are better done by you as well as that which must be done by you. Some of the "better" category needs to be entrusted to others.

A good executive secretary may be a better choice than another leader like you. A good secretary is better for tasks that are routine. Interruptions can be controlled and many things presently done by the leader can be performed by a good secretary. A secretary might be able to meet the needs of several leaders, and thus, not only help you, but others.

Be careful about hiring an assistant to help you. That suggests that you cannot do your job and need help. It also makes you the "growth-restricting" obstacle. The assistant is limited by your direction and approval. To view him as an "associate" is better. You are partners even though you may have the final decision on major matters. It is better to delegate areas of ministry to another leader than specific jobs that fall under your area of ministry. Maybe the new leader you've hired will do things differently than you and even do them better. Give him total responsibility in a given area of ministry and let him run with it. Let him rise and fall by himself. He will grow faster and appreciate you more.

Disunity is a heavy burden for a leader to bear. Loyalty and love are the two most important ingredients among people who work together. Disunity can greatly affect the leader's motivations. In a desire to solve the problem, leaders can act too hastily or without proper information and facts.

A fellow co-worker spoke to me one day about what he thought was disloyalty on the part of another worker. The worker was doing something that I do not do and which appeared to be disloyal. The one who shared it with me did not realize that I had told that person what I would do but that he could do whatever he wanted. I trusted him completely. He was not disloyal; he was simply doing it another way which proved to be more effective than the way I usually handle that situation.

When real disunity and disloyalty (not hearsay or someone's opinions) occur, how should you handle the problem? These things have helped me in those difficult situations and times of tension and stress.

(1) Identify the problem—make sure you have the facts clearly; (2) Learn to face it and deal with it. It just doesn't go away by itself; (3) Recognize the real source of the problem (see Jas. 3:14-16; 4:1); (4) Express love to all concerned and seek their best interest; (5) Be willing to listen to all sides and viewpoints; (6) Emphasize prayer, confidence in God and getting things right with Him first; (7) Be tolerant and forgiving, seek to restore rather than sever relationships; (8) Thank God for the problem. He has allowed it, so learn from it; (9) Determine whether the situation demands the removal of a staff member. If the disloyalty continues after confrontation, then the removal must happen or other serious problems will develop.

Every situation is, of course, different. Leaders need the wisdom of God. If I put my finger on the problem that most often occurs, it is the failure of leaders to deal quickly with situations that arise. We hope they will go away. My experience tells me differently. Deal with them in love as soon as possible.

Leaders are not exempt from having personal problems. Things like bad health, financial difficulty, marital disharmony, bad relationships in the family, or with other people, can all affect your motivations and your peace of mind. The pressure of these things can be so great upon you that it starts affecting your leadership, and it becomes noticeable by others around you who work with you. How do you handle this?

Begin by thanking God for the problems you're having (see Phil. 4:6,7) and seeking His wisdom and help through prayer and study of the Word. Don't seek sympathy from others all the time. If you can't handle the problems, how can others who follow your leadership expect to handle theirs? Also, don't publicly refer to your personal problems. If people ask you in loving concern, then you might want to respond. But, don't parade your personal troubles before others. It will hinder their reaction to you as a leader. It will keep them from wanting your help in time of need. Learn the principle that your personal problems are intended by God to help you share with compassion with others. Problems are designed to help you learn the secret of God's strength (see 2 Cor. 12:7-10). If you don't have problems, you're not human.

Hebrews 5:1,2 speaks about priests being chosen from among men so that they can deal gently with the ignorant and misguided, since they also are beset with weaknesses. People will not come to you for help if you are not human. They must understand that you know by experience what they are experiencing. This identification with people is vital to the role of spiritual leadership.

What Motives Should Spiritual Leaders Have?

In order to do things for the right reasons we need to have proper and biblical motives. The problems will be there and we have to face them. We cannot run away from problems. It's a part of what leadership is all about. But, we need to do things from proper motives. God will bless that. Our leadership will grow when the heart is right.

It all starts with the glory of God. First Corinthians 10:31 says to do everything to the glory of God. Whatever you do as a leader, ask yourself this one question, "Will this glorify God?" To glorify God is to honor and praise Him. It means to give Him all the credit.

The spiritual leader must constantly seek to win the lost to Christ. He is to be all things to all men that we might by some means save a few (see 1 Cor. 9:19-22). He knows that the Great Commission is his job. He does not justify his obedience to Christ on the basis of his work with the saved. His work must also include the desire to win as many people to Christ as he possibly can.

Good leaders will seek to maintain balance in their leadership between the ministry with the believer and their evangelism of the nonbeliever. Frequently, leaders need to ask of what they do, "What is contributing to the salvation of lost people?" Determine what ministries are designed for the purpose of evangelism. If none exists, then the spiritual leadership is lacking in that organization.

Most evangelistic efforts in Christian organizations are designed to invite nonbelievers to attend meetings where believers are accustomed to go. If you want to penetrate your community for Christ, design efforts that are attractive to nonbelievers: Try a "Self-protection Clinic" for the women of the community with Christian police officers conducting it and sharing the gospel during it; put on a men's breakfast (without charge) in a non-church environment (like a local restaurant), with a sports personality who loves Christ and knows how to communicate with nonbelievers; have your young people provide a free car wash to the people of the community with appropriate gospel literature and witness; establish some special seminars in marriage and family subjects that will appeal to nonbelievers and be especially designed to reach them.

Above all, learn to go where the people are, instead of expecting them to come to you. Reach out to them where they live and speak their language. Provide services for them, like counseling, or day care centers. Constantly evaluate what you do as to how many contacts you are making with nonbelievers. The more contacts, the better the opportunities to win people to Christ.

It is wise to provide a program of training for the believers in how to share their faith. This program should be carried on as a regular part of your ministry, thus emphasizing to everyone the priority of evangelism in the motives behind your leadership.

Paul said he worked hard at the maturity of believers (see Col. 1:28,29). Spiritual leaders are to equip the believers for ministry (see Eph. 4:11,12). Sometimes we use people to build our work rather than using our work to build people. The difference is enormous in terms of motivation! Keep emphasizing maturity and spiritual growth. Make sure what you do contributes to it. Seek to build up rather than tear down.

One day in a staff meeting we were evaluating a certain project. It seemed like a good idea and everyone was leaning toward it until one of the brothers asked what it would do to encourage the spiritual growth of our people. Silence. It was obviously not a project for evangelism, and it did not seem too valuable in developing maturity among our people. Then, why were we doing it? So much for a good idea! We went on to something else.

One more word about maturity. Make sure that the growth you are talking about is spiritual. We are to grow in the grace and knowledge of Jesus Christ (see 2 Pet. 3:18).

Serve out of the love of Christ. There are two ways to look at this motive. One is our love for Christ and what He's done for us. The other is His love for us, displayed through what He did at the cross. Second Corinthians 5:14 seems to take the latter view. Christ died for us, thus demonstrating His love for us. That love He had for us at the cross motivates us or constrains us. He stimulates us to proper action by His love for us. That is the way it should be. We work better under conditions where love prevails.

When His love is compelling and controlling us, we will also love others (see 1 John 4:7ff). Most employees in Christian organizations expect the level of love to be greater than secular employment. That's only natural. A great deal of disappointment hits the Christian worker when the atmosphere resembles what he knew in the world. It need not be that way. Christians indwelt by the Holy Spirit have the capacity to love each other with God's love. Love is a tremendous motivating factor. More about this in a later chapter.

A heavenly reward is motivation for service. Some feel this is not a worthy motive. However, Paul taught in 1 Corinthians 9:24-27 that the thought of an imperishable crown in the future was a motivating factor to the way he conducted his life. Jesus reminded us (see Matt. 6:19-21) about laying up treasures in heaven and not on earth. Second Corinthians 5:10 states that we must all appear before the judgment seat of Christ. What believer has not been motivated by the thought of hearing Jesus say, "Well done, good and faithful servant; enter into the joy of the Lord" (see Matt. 25:21).

It is important for the spiritual leader to do things for the right reasons. It affects the response of people as well as their respect. There are problems that beset the leader, causing him at times to slip back to an unworthy motive. We all fail at times. It's a reminder to all spiritual leaders of their need of depending upon the Lord. May God help all of us to do things His way!

Leader's Checklist

1. Have you considered why you have such few results? List some possible reasons.

2. Can you handle criticism from others without being discouraged? Think of some recent instances when you have been criticized. How did you handle it?

3. Do you know why people do not cooperate? List some possible reasons.

4. What do you do to meet the need of loneliness in your life?

5. Do you understand the importance of friends? How many close friends do you have? Name them. Do they know they are your close friends?

6. Why do you take on heavy work loads?

7. Would a secretary be a better assistant to you than another leader like yourself?

8. What steps would you take to deal with disunity and disloyalty?

9. Do you constantly refer to personal problems in your life? To whom?

10. Which of your motives are biblical and spiritual?

PART V

**AUTHORITY:
WILL PEOPLE
RESPOND TO YOUR
LEADERSHIP?**

WHY DO PEOPLE RESIST AUTHORITY?

It's natural to resist authority! But knowing that doesn't always provide spiritual leaders with practical answers to practical problems. Interpersonal relationships in any Christian organization are affected greatly by the concepts of authority which are held by those people.

A pastor friend told me of his desire to "straighten out" a church that had a history of short pastorates. The problem, he said, was a lack of authority. People did not respond to the authority of the previous pastors. He was going to change all that. He lasted six months.

Sometimes the reason people are resisting is found in the life of the leader. At other times, it doesn't matter who the leader is, the problem of resistance is built into the people.

One example of resistance to authority happened in a church with which I am acquainted. The church had been established for about 25 years previous to its sale. During those 25 years the church had several pastors, none of whom was the authority. One man who had invested great sums of money into the work from the beginning became a kind of spiritual godfather. He had the legal papers for the church in his home, and the keys to the building. What he said in the meetings of that church was considered to be right. No questions asked. When the church started to decline, no one realized that the problem was this man. They blamed it on different pastors. Finally, the church declined all the way down to this one man. Everyone else left. Sad.

This problem of authority is enormous, but very few want to deal with it or bring any understanding to the many Christian organizations that face it.

Webster's dictionary lists the following meaning of the word "authority":

1. Legal or rightful power; a right to command or to act; jurisdiction.

2. A person, board, or commission having power in a particular field.

3. Government; those exercising power or command.

4. One claimed, or appealed to, in support of opinions, actions, measures, etc; hence:

    a. Testimony; witness.

    b. A precedent; previous decision of a court.

    c. A book or its author.

    d. Justification; warrant.

5. Power due to opinion or esteem; influence of character, station, mental or moral superiority, or the like.

As these definitions are examined, they seem to describe what most people would say about authority. The problem with all of these definitions deals with the source or basis of all authority. What is the ultimate authority? If a so-called "authority" must present its credentials to another individual, group, or institution, it cannot be the ultimate authority. If our "right" to authority is given to us, then we are not the ultimate authority.

Problems in Society that Cause
Resistance to Authority

Today people question authority (and authorities) more than ever. Some have called our society a "crisis in authority." There is a breakdown in authority and the exercising of it in every realm of society, including schools, churches, businesses, and government (at all levels). There is little respect for authority, and the rights of the individual are exalted to the exclusion of authority which makes those rights possible in the first place. What has gone wrong? Why are people not responding to authority? Why do most people question the right to rule and lead? Why do leaders have such a difficult time dealing with those under their leadership? Here are a few reasons people give.

The failure of the previous generation to discipline their children. When there is no consistent pattern of discipline on the part of the parents toward their children, there develops a spirit of rebellion. Proverbs 29:15 says, "The rod and reproof give wisdom, but a child who gets his own way brings shame to his mother." Proverbs 29:17 adds, "Correct your son, and he will give you comfort; He will also delight your soul." Proverbs 22:6 shows us the importance of the parental responsibility when it states: "Train up a child in the way he should go, even when he is old he will not depart from it." Proverbs 19:18 points out the need to discipline early: "Discipline your son while there is hope, and do not desire his death." Parents who argue that they love their children too much to discipline them are only proving the opposite. Proverbs 13:24 makes that clear: "He who spares his rod hates his son, but he who loves him disciplines him diligently." The reason why the child needs discipline is recorded in Proverbs 22:15: "Foolishness is bound up in the heart of a child; the rod of discipline will remove it far from him." Perhaps the following chart will help us in seeing how the discipline of children is related to respect and response to authority.

	Discipline	Punishment
Purpose	To develop maturity by correction	To inflict penalty for an offense
Focus	Future correct deeds	Past misdeeds
Parents' Attitudes	Love/concern	Hostility/anger/frustration
Child's Emotions	Security and trust	Fear and guilt
Child's Future Conduct	Submission/respect toward authority	Rebellion to authority

A child that grows up under the "punishment" concept will manifest a resistance to authority much more than the one who is properly disciplined. The lack of any discipline can also prove damaging to the attitudes of the child in later life. If the parents give the child everything the child wants or demands, there is every possibility that there will be a resistance to authority later in the child's life.

A man came to my office one day to talk about one of his employees, who was a Christian but was failing to submit to authority. This employer wanted to do the right thing. I had an opportunity to talk with the rebellious young man and discovered that he viewed his employer like he was his father. His father never disciplined him, and in his childhood he always got his parents to respond by throwing a tantrum, or making a scene. The young man had hostile attitudes toward his employer and was extremely upset that he could not get his own way at work as he had at home when he was growing up. My advice to him was to submit to authority or lose his job. He responded well, fortunately.

Many of the problems in leadership can be traced to improper discipline in the homes of the people who now must work together. The real solution to this problem is to go back to basics in the home. Teach and discipline according to God's Word. The immediate problems at work can be solved only by the person's recognition of the problem and a willingness to be submissive to authority. That will take the power and control of the Holy Spirit. For a person to overcome years of improper discipline in his home is not impossible, but is difficult. A pattern of submission to God and authority can overcome the pattern of resistance and rebellion.

The failure of society to teach moral absolutes. It is not difficult to understand how this problem affects the matter of authority. A relative standard of morality will lead one to a humanistic philosophy where the "self" is the authority and the one determining what is morally right or wrong. Today's society which says, "If it feels good, do it," has concluded that the person responsible for determining the morality of any word or action is none other than yourself! We are often told that if everyone agrees to it, then that makes it right. Or, if at least the majority has voted it, then it is right!

Without moral absolutes, there must inevitably be a breakdown in authority and people's response to it. An illustration of this can be found in Romans 10:3. Paul says, "For not knowing about God's righteousness, and seeking to establish their own, they did not subject themselves to the righteousness of God."

In the intellectual atmosphere of today's colleges and universities, every statement and axiom can be questioned. Nothing is ever regarded as being true or not true, right or wrong. The answer today is, "It all depends!" Morality is flexible, depending on the situation or condition of things involved. The mood of most people is that they do not want anyone telling them what to do or that something *must* be done. That suggests a certain moral "oughtness," or moral requirement, and that demands a moral authority behind it! People say, "Who says so?" Or, "Who does he think he is?" Or, "What makes him think he is the authority around here?" The atmosphere of rebellion and resistance is thriving in what many call a "moral vacuum."

The failure of institutions of learning to teach leadership and principles of authority. No doubt some of the blame can be placed here. Authority, leadership, and management are subjects of great interest to many people, but the way these great subjects are taught in most institutions leaves many in doubt and question about assuming the role of leadership. To be in a place of authority today involves much criticism and attack. Many point to the way the schools are teaching. The rights of the individual have been exalted to the point that those in authority always appear to be the "bad guys." Attacks upon people in authority are frequent in college and university classrooms. Everyone seems to be "in it for themselves." People cheat and lie, and have no qualms about disobeying the law. If you can get away with it, it seems to be all right to do it. No wonder there is a crisis in authority today!

The failure of those in authority to be examples before others. Scandals in the lives of those in authority have a tendency to weaken the people's response to authority. If a leader's life does not back up what he says, then he can hardly be trusted and relied upon in the matter of exercising his authority. This is certainly a valid criticism, and some of the blame must rest upon the shoulders of those in positions of authority. Proverbs 29:2 says, "When the righteous increase, the people rejoice, but when a wicked man rules, people groan." The New Testament places great emphasis upon the qualifications of those in positions of leadership—they are to be examples. Of course, such moral conduct assumes that there are moral absolutes upon which to make our evaluations and these absolutes have moral authority.

In speaking about false teachers and ungodly leaders, the Bible says, in 2 Peter 2:9,10, "The Lord knows how to rescue the godly from temptation, and to keep the unrighteous under punishment for the day of judgment, and especially those who indulge the flesh in its corrupt desires and *despise authority*" (italics added). Jude adds in verse 8 of his book: "Yet in the same manner these men also by dreaming defile the flesh, and *reject authority*" (italics added). The characteristics of these false teachers is the despising and rejecting of authority.

The natural tendency of each individual toward rebellion. Some do not like to admit or acknowledge this truth that is found in the Bible over and over again— man is sinful, and his actions are controlled by a sinful and selfish nature with which he was born. David said in Psalm 51:5, "Behold, I was brought forth in iniquity, and in sin my mother conceived me." Ephesians 2:1-3 graphically portrays this problem: "And you were dead in your trespasses and sins, in which you formerly walked according to the course of this world, according to the prince of the power of the air, of the spirit that is now working in the sons of disobedience. Among them we too all formerly lived in the lusts of our flesh, indulging the desires of the flesh and of the mind, and were *by nature* children of wrath, even as the rest."

First John 1:8 and 10 say: "If we say that we have no

114

sin, we are deceiving ourselves, and the truth is not in us . . . . If we say that we have not sinned, we make Him a liar, and His word is not in us." It seems very clear that the problem is not merely that of parents, authorities, institutions, standards of morality in society, or anything that is outside of man, the problem is in our own hearts! We are "rebels" by nature! We are prone toward self and sin, not submission to godly authority.

We do not want anyone telling us what to do—it is against our nature! Romans 1:21-23 describes the human dilemma: "For even though they knew God, they did not honor Him as God, or give thanks; but they became futile in their speculations, and their foolish heart was darkened. Professing to be wise, they became fools, and exchanged the glory of the incorruptible God for an image in the form of corruptible man and of birds and four-footed animals and crawling creatures." Romans 1:30 adds, "Slanderers, haters of God, insolent, arrogant, boastful, inventors of evil, disobedient to parents." Second Timothy 3:1-5 describes the last days and tells us that men will be "boastful, arrogant, revilers, disobedient to parents . . . . " Yes, the problem is in the human heart. We are sinners by nature and act.

When describing God's principles and teaching concerning the practice of immorality in 1 Thessalonians 4:1-8, there is a fascinating statement in verse 8 that concerns us in the discussion of authority. It says, "Consequently, he who rejects this is not rejecting man but the God who gives His Holy Spirit to you." The point here is that our rebellion and rejection is primarily directed toward God Himself.

Thank God that there is a solution for the rebellion in the heart of all of us! Our sin has been paid for by the precious blood of Jesus Christ, and salvation is made possible through His work on the cross and His resurrection. It demands our faith in what Christ has done for us, not in what we can do for Him. We must believe on the Lord Jesus Christ in order to be saved.

When we are "born again" we receive a new nature from God that is inclined toward Him. This new nature is in constant conflict with our old nature (which will not be removed until the coming of Christ). The understanding and response toward authority should be much greater among believers than among nonbelievers. Believers can, of course, allow their old sin natures to dominate and become what the Bible calls "carnal."

Christian organizations can experience great disunity, disloyalty, and rebellion to authority if the sin natures of those employed there are not controlled by the Holy Spirit. The secret to an effective organization where there is response and respect toward authority is a Spirit-filled life. One part of the fruit of the Spirit is "self-control." When we are controlled by the Holy Spirit, we will not carry out the desires of the flesh (including rebellion and failure to submit to authority), according to Galatians 5:16.

Organizational Problems that Can Cause Resistance to Authority

In addition to the basic problem of the old sin nature and the failures of parents, society, institutions, etc., there are some practical problems in every organization that can lead to authority problems. Spotting these early and doing something about them can save the leader many heartaches.

No job descriptions. When people do not know what to do, they get frustrated and resist authority. When the lines of responsibility are not clearly drawn in job descriptions, people have a tendency to get into one another's hair! There is overlapping and attitudes like,

116

"That's not my job," or "Nobody told me to do that," or "That's your problem, not mine."

Job descriptions must start at the top. Until we know what the chief leader is to do, we cannot design the jobs immediately under him. A job description does not need to be lengthy or too detailed. It should deal with basics: what is expected, to whom responsible, for whom responsible, limits of authority, etc.

No follow-through by the leadership. This is a common complaint. When a person submits a request to the leadership and it is ignored or neglected, attitudes of resistance develop immediately. Leaders must learn to follow through on matters that affect their people.

One of our staff members was becoming resistant and it was starting to show. In dealing with the problem, I learned that I was the problem. He had submitted plans to me that had not been acted upon, nor had he been informed of what I was doing about it. He deserved to be upset. He should be submissive at all times, but his reaction was understandable.

No explanations. When no explanations are given for decisions that affect the majority of people who work for you, attitudes of resistance begin to develop. Leaders must learn to share with people as to why they are doing what they are doing. Everyone will not agree, but they'll all be happy their opinions were heard or that the leader was willing to explain. When the people who work for you are the last ones to hear about decisions that are made, they feel neglected and that the leadership does not value them too highly.

It seemed like a simple matter—moving a few offices around, relocating people, without explanation. You guessed it, I had problems! I wound up explaining in some detail to every person involved in the moves! It was my fault, not theirs. Though the matter seemed small to me, it was not at all inconsequential to them.

Showing partiality. This will do it every time! Just start paying one staff member more than another at the same level, and you'll see some resistance to authority. Give one staff member a nicer office than another who serves at the same level of responsibility, and you'll have problems, unless everyone is agreeable, loving, and willing. Of course, if your offices are all different, then you'll have to make some decisions that won't please everybody, but taking time to talk it over can sure help!

Showing partiality can be seen in the amount of time spent by the leader with a particular staff person, especially when it's not company business. People are very sensitive, and leaders must be understanding toward how the people feel. Leaders must show love and concern for all, without partiality.

Demanding extra work without asking. When a leader simply tells an employee what he wants them to do and it is not a part of the person's regular job, an attitude of resistance can easily develop. The employee begins to feel the leader does not really care or understand his feelings. Naturally, employees should be willing to submit to the employer's demands (the Bible teaches this), but spiritual leaders will do themselves a favor if they stop demanding and begin asking.

If a leader needs an employee to stay and work extra hours, he should ask, not demand. A question like, "Would it be possible for you to help me complete this by staying after work today?" is much better than "You'll have to stay after work today to complete this project." When the leader wants an employee to do work that is not a part of that person's job, it's better to say, "Would you be able to help me on this; I know it's not your job, but I really need help!" than to say, "Have this done as soon as you can!"

The leader who works like this is building for the future. People will respond more quickly to your needs when they know you are asking, not demanding. Maybe you have a right to demand, but if you think about it, the level of productivity might be higher when there is an atmosphere of love and kindness.

One final thing about this: Make sure you express your sincere thanks for the extra effort. Gratefulness leads to better response. One of the most forgotten forms of worker's compensation is the phrase, "Thank you very much." It means much more than money!

Organizational problems can cause resistance to authority. Don't let them continue. Learn to deal with them quickly. People respond to leaders who care about them and their feelings.

Leader's Checklist

1. Do certain people resist your authority? Who are they? Have you discovered why?
2. How would you handle someone who resisted your authority?
3. Is your example before others such that people can respond favorably to your authority? Why?
4. Do you have an adequate job description for yourself? For your co-workers? Are these in writing?
5. Do you always respond immediately to the requests of others?
6. Do you take time to explain your decisions when they affect others? Describe a recent situation when you did this.
7. Do you ever show partiality? Name a recent instance.
8. Do you have a habit of demanding rather than asking? What is the difference?

10
HOW DO YOU GET AUTHORITY?

Authority is essential to the effective operation of any organization. It exists whether it is recognized or not. It often lies in a corner unnoticed by those with titles and offices. How does a person get authority? Where does it come from?

The Source of Authority

Without God, there is no moral foundation for authority. Without God, it is impossible to establish moral rightness. Everything is relative and situational without God. There are no absolutes without God.

Before anything else existed, there was God. The Bible does not set out to prove His existence, it assumes it. The One who created us has the right to tell us what to do. Every authority in the world is accountable for the exercise of that authority to God Himself. Many management problems could be cleared up if this principle were recognized and applied.

The Bible teaches that God is king over all and His Kingdom includes everything and everyone (see Dan. 4:3,34; 6:26; 7:14). King David said (see 1 Chron. 29:11,12) that God was the head over all, and that He rules over all. Everything comes from Him. Romans 9:21 says He is the potter and we are the clay; He has a right to form us the way He wants. Psalm 24 reminds us that the earth and all it contains belong to the Lord. Romans 11:36 says all things come from Him, are being worked through Him, and have Him as their ultimate goal. Psalm 103:19 tells us that God's sovereignty rules over all.

God has also determined the levels of authority that exist in society. God the Father gave special authority to His Son, Jesus Christ (see John 17:2). Christ's authority affects many areas of our lives. In marriage, Christ is the head of every husband, and the husband the head of his wife. In the church, Christ is the head. In business, employers are reminded (see Eph. 6:9) of their Master in heaven.

God's authority is expressed clearly in the written pages of the Bible, making the Bible the number one manual on authority. The Bible rings with authority in statements like "Thus says the Lord" and "The Word of the Lord came to me, saying." The Bible demands our obedience and submission to what it says. The reason it can do that is because it is God's Word. God is the ultimate source of all authority.

One of the major problems in establishing the principle of authority in a person's life is his relationship to God. If he does not recognize God as the ultimate source of all authority, he will see no need of submitting to levels of authority which God in His Word has established.

God has established authority in marriage, family, government, business, and the church. The believer is exhorted to submit to the authorities that God has established.

One of the keys to having authority is learning to

submit. It almost seems to be an axiom that the degree of authority in a person's life is directly traceable to the amount of submission to the authorities which God has placed in that person's life. If you cannot submit to authority yourself, you cannot expect others to submit to you. God promises to exalt the one who learns to submit (see Jas. 4:10).

Much of the problem in responding to authority lies in the mistaken ideas people have about authority. These ideas often control a person's response even though he is unaware of it.

Mistaken Ideas of Authority

Some of the problems people have in working well with others and being under the leadership of others is due to the mistaken ideas of authority they have been accustomed to. Following are some of these mistaken ideas.

Authority comes from what a person feels in himself. We often speak of "authoritarian" figures—people who seem to have innate authority. They feel it, and others around them feel the same thing. This authority can arise from the way people talk, dress, or relate to others. It is imaginary authority, not real. It is imagined by the individual himself or others around him. It sometimes results from a sense of pride and self-confidence. It can also stem from insecurity which causes the person to manifest "authoritarian" attitudes and actions. How long and loudly we talk sometimes reveals our insecurity and pride.

Authority is an acquired ability to rule. This mistaken idea assumes that the exercise of authority can be learned or acquired by the individual who aspires to it. People who believe this will spend time reading and studying the principles of management and authority and believe that this knowledge gives them the right or the ability to exercise authority over others. Sometimes this mistaken idea is based on that which a person has bought or inherited. There is a very real sense in which he who owns is he who has authority. However, merely owning cannot guarantee effective authority—especially in the matter of spiritual leadership. You may have the power that money can bring, but it does not mean that you have spiritual leadership or authority.

Authority is based on the will of the majority. This is a common belief among people and represents the "democratic" way of doing things. The trouble is that voting someone into a position of authority does not, of itself, bring that authority. If 100 people vote for a leader and 51 say yes and 49 say no, the person is elected. This particular example reveals the danger of this method of establishing authority. To compensate for this problem, many religious organizations insist on a two-thirds majority in selecting leaders. This is no guarantee that a spiritual leader has been chosen or that spiritual authority will be exercised.

This method is often based on popularity or the person who is best known and offers the least problems. In order for this process to be used, other factors must be considered first, which will be discussed shortly. It is very possible for the majority to be wrong. When people are not Spirit-filled or living godly lives or basing their opinions on biblical standards, it will be very difficult for them to make the right decisions.

Authority is based on the acceptance of others. This view contains a very important truth: When no one responds to an individual's authority, there will be questions about that person's ability to manage or rule. But, it is no guarantee that a person is not a leader because people do not respond. A wife is to respond to her

123

husband's authority regardless of whether he is properly exercising it. This is true of the responsibility of children to parents, employees to employers, etc. The problem may rest with the attitudes of those under that authority. Their past record of subjection may also affect their response to authority.

Many leaders are looking to those under them for assurance of their position and authority. This kind of leader is extremely insecure and will continue to be so until he discovers the real basis of authority. He will have a tendency to compromise and tolerate situations that ought not to exist simply because he does not want to offend people under him, people whose response brings him assurance of his authority.

Authority is based on the office or title given. This is so prevalent in society today, one wonders when it is going to be challenged and buried. It appeals to human pride to have a particular title or office and thus feel important and authoritative. All the lofty titles in the world cannot give you the authority that God describes in His Word.

Promotion is a key motivating factor in the business world today, especially when a larger salary and greater benefits are involved. Sometimes we let these "crutches" support us in believing we have a measure of authority, but real authority is based on different principles.

It is important at times to have titles that represent the work a person does, but when it is used to give the person a sense of authority, it is a waste of time. Real authority does not come by merely giving a person a title. Nor does it come by the kind of office he has or his physical surroundings. The size of an office or its elaborate furnishings is often the way people determine the "executives." This is foolish, and in no way represents real authority! It is not a bad idea for executives to move offices from time to time to teach this principle. It is also a good idea for an executive to give his office to a person with less authority and take a smaller office for himself. If more executives would do this, there would be less problems of interpersonal relationships and more understanding of what real authority is all about. Maybe those who design offices (especially in Christian organizations) should make them all identical in size and furnishings!

The Basis of Spiritual Authority

Spiritual authority is based on factors which God Himself reveals in His written Word. Your ability to have great influence upon the lives of others is dependent upon these factors. The influence that God wants you to accomplish and exercise toward others is built upon what you, as a person, are really like. Your reputation is what people think you are; your character is what God knows you to be. More could be said about these factors, and no doubt, more factors could be added to this list. Hopefully, these few principles will guide all of us into a true understanding of authority.

Authority is based on submission to God Himself. James 4:7 says, "Submit therefore to God." Verse 10 says, "Humble yourselves in the presence of the Lord, and He will exalt you." The way up is the way down! Humility and submission are the foundation of authority. The amount of spiritual authority in our lives is directly in proportion to our humility and submission to God and His Word. There will be many tests along the way to see what our submission to God is like. There will be times when we will be tempted to compromise or violate God's Word for a moment's pleasure or profit. Those times are the keys to the spiritual authority we will exercise. If we are not submissive to God, the chances are that those under our authority will not submit to us.

Authority is based on a godly life-style. Hebrews 13:7 says, "Remember those who led you, who spoke the word of God to you; and considering the outcome of their way of life, imitate their faith." Notice that the response of the followers to what the leaders say is based on the conduct of those leaders. The phrase, "Practice what you preach," is constantly emphasized in the Scriptures. Leaders who cannot be trusted and respected in terms of godly life-style will have very little spiritual authority in the lives of others. Paul wrote in 1 Thessalonians 1:5, "For our gospel did not come to you in word only, but also in power and in the Holy Spirit and with full conviction; just as you know what kind of men we proved to be among you for your sake." He said in chapter 2, verses 3-6: "For our exhortation does not come from error or impurity or by way of deceit; but just as we have been approved by God to be entrusted with the gospel, so we speak, not as pleasing men but God, who examines our hearts. For we never came with flattering speech, as you know, nor with a pretext for greed —God is witness—nor did we seek glory from men, either from you or from others, even though as apostles of Christ we might have asserted our authority."

Authority is based on your love for people. People respond best to loving authority. Children respond to the authority of parents when it is backed by love and concern. Discipline without love can produce rebellion rather than submission. In 1 Thessalonians 2:3-12, Paul spoke about his authority and influence among these believers. In contrasting his style with the wrong motives of others, he said in verses 7 and 8: "But we proved to be gentle among you, *as a nursing mother tenderly*

126

cares for her own children. Having thus a fond affection for you, we were well pleased to impart to you not only the gospel but also our own lives, because you had become very dear to us," In verse 11, he adds: "Just as you know how we were exhorting and encouraging and imploring each one of you *as a father would his own children*" (italics added in both passages). Your loving concern for others will increase your authority and influence in their lives.

Authority is based on a servant's heart. Jesus referred to the kind of authority that the rulers of the Gentiles use. In Mark 10:42 He spoke of how they "lord it over them." But His kind of spiritual authority is different. He said in verses 43-45: "But it is not so among you, but whoever wishes to become great among you shall be your servant; and whoever wishes to be first among you shall be slave of all. For even the Son of Man did not come to be served, but to serve, and to give His life a ransom for many." Our desire and willingness to serve others is a key to our spiritual authority. Spiritual leaders will seek to make those who work under them more effective. They will serve them in every way possible; they will try to make conditions and situations affecting their work as pleasant as possible. They will give them opportunities and challenges to grow and develop under their leadership without trying to suppress that growth for selfish reasons.

Ways to Get Authority

Spiritual authority is the most important kind of authority. This does not mean that other kinds of authorities are not important or real. A husband is the authority in his marriage. That is real authority, but not necessarily spiritual authority. A wife is to respond to her husband's authority even when he is not obeying God's

Word (see 1 Pet. 3:1-6). However, her response and his blessing will be so much better when the husband's authority is also spiritual authority, based on the principles we have just shared.

So, in what ways can a person get authority? These thoughts are very practical and come out of the arena of personal experience. They are in addition to what was said about spiritual authority. When we are placed into positions of authority in any one of these areas or through any one of these ways, we should then seek to have spiritual authority in all we do and say.

Authority comes through decisions you make. When you decide to get married, you (if a man) automatically become the authority in your marriage. It is a position which God has previously established. When you decide to have children, you automatically become the authority as a parent. When you decide to apply for a job, and you are hired, a measure of authority accompanies the job you have received.

Authority comes through delegation by others. When your employer gives you authority, it comes to you by delegation. Your authority exists because of his authority. The way you use it may determine the extent of your authority in the lives of others, but nonetheless, you have a measure of authority because it was given to you.

Authority exists when you established or started a ministry. Whenever a person develops something from the beginning, it is his baby. Authority exists because he brought it into existence. He must make the decisions as to the transfer of authority to others. This is a matter of prior claim. He has a claim upon that ministry because he began it.

When an attempt is made to change the authority in an organization or particular ministry without the consent of the one who founded it, inevitably there are

128

problems. It is better to start a new ministry, than to change the old without approval of the one who started it.

This truth applies to a group as well as an individual. When a group establishes a brand new ministry, and another group comes along and tries to change things, immediately there is conflict and deep problems in authority. Organizations can be changed when the authority is properly transferred. Otherwise, a new ministry must be established.

Authority comes through financial support. This can be a dangerous problem in authority. Money does buy power, whether we like it or not. A wise leader will do all he can to keep people from exercising authority because of financial support.

If you bought something with your own money, then the purchase grants you a measure of authority over that item. The principle of private property is involved here. If you buy a piece of land and it belongs to you, then you have the authority in determining the future of it.

In Christian ministry, believers must be careful to support God's work with their financial resources without desiring authority in the use of their money. Charitable contributions should have no strings attached.

A gift is not a right to exercise authority. A gift should be based on love, not a desire to control another person or organization.

Authority comes through experience. If you have had great experience in some area of ministry, you will be looked to for advice and expertise. You become an authority because you know what you are talking about.

It becomes a problem when your experience becomes the final word. When you are not open to new ideas, your past experience can irritate people rather than help them. Statements like, "It won't work; we tried that before!" or "We've always done it this way!" can seriously endanger your authority before others.

Experiences can deepen your authority when you apply them to situations that prove wise and helpful. The more your past experience helps those in the present, the greater will be your authority.

Remember, the greatest authority is spiritual authority. Make sure that the authority you concentrate on is that which produces spiritual results and gives glory to God.

Leader's Checklist

1. Have you properly established your relationship to God as the ultimate source of all authority? Describe how you see this happening.
2. Is submitting to God's authority a problem in your life?
3. Review the section "Mistaken Ideas of Authority." Do you recognize any of these problems in your life? Which ones need your immediate attention?
4. On a scale of 1-10 how do you rate yourself in being submissive to God?

1	2	3	4	5	6	7	8	9	10
Rebellious									Submissive

5. On a scale of 1-10 how do you rate yourself on having a godly life-style?

1	2	3	4	5	6	7	8	9	10
Worldly Life-style									Godly Life-style

6. Do you really love the people you lead? How are they able to tell?
7. How willing are you to be a servant to others?
8. Review the section "Ways to Get Authority." If you are in a position of authority, how did you get there?
9. Do you give glory to God for spiritual results?

PART VI

**STRATEGY:
DO YOU KNOW
WHERE YOU
ARE GOING?**

GOOD LEADERS HAVE A STRATEGY

Aim at nothing, and you'll hit it every time! We've all heard that from time to time, but its truth sinks into the hearts of very few, unfortunately! Do you know where you're going? Leaders must have a strategy. They must know how to get things done.

A good strategy is composed of the following five things:

- *Objectives*—the basic purposes of the organization.
- *Goals*—the specific ways in which the purposes of the organization will be measured and accomplished.
- *Priorities*—the factors that determine when and why things are done.
- *Planning*—the process used to achieve the goals (includes personnel, resources, obstacles, and evaluation).
- *Guidelines*—the moral and ethical framework in which the organization will seek to accomplish its goals.

Organizations should have a philosophy of ministry which includes these five things. Every leader within that organization should be reminded of these things frequently. It is so easy to get sidetracked and off the main objectives and specific goals. It is the leader's responsibility to keep things on the right track.

Why Do We Need a Strategy?

Many organizations and leaders are operating without a good strategy. They have only one goal in mind and that is to keep the organization going from day to day. They deal only with present problems and needs. Organizations like that have "a terminal illness." If not "terminal" it is at least "sick." An organization is not healthy that does not know where it is going and why.

Consider some of the reasons why you need a good strategy. Perhaps they will uncover some basic causes for frustration, confusion, and lack of enthusiasm and growth within your organization.

Without a strategy, we don't know why we are doing what we are doing. An organization may provide employment for people and may design specific jobs for people to do. But, if a strategy is missing, a person's reason for working diminishes. This is especially true in Christian organizations. There is a certain idealism in the heart of every believer who goes to work for a Christian organization. That person wants to be a part of something really great, something that will count for eternity. He or she likes to feel that the work is being done for the Lord. And rightly so. At some point, when the Christian worker begins to ask why a certain thing is being done, the strategy is then vital. An explanation is needed. The worker needs to be motivated by the high and lofty goals of the organization. Otherwise, why not get another job in a secular institution (the pay is probably better anyway)?

One of our secretaries was discouraged. We chatted together one day about her work. She had lost sight of how what she was doing fit into the important objectives

133

and goals of the church. When she was reminded of them, tears came to her eyes. She realized the importance of her work once again. She was grateful to be a part of it. It wasn't the money that motivated her. I learned an important lesson.

Without a strategy, we lose interest in what we are doing. Without objectives and goals in an organization, it is easy to lose interest. It becomes more difficult to go into the office each day. Work is not exciting anymore. It's boring and dull. You begin to feel apathetic, indifferent to pressing needs and responsibilities. When this happens, the leader should take a good look at the strategy. Is there one? What does it say? Is it up to date?

One of our staff members was losing interest in a particular area of ministry. It was obvious to everyone around him. He knew the overall strategy of the organization, but he had not applied that to his area of ministry. Attendance had been declining in recent months. When reminded again of the importance of a strategy in every area of ministry, he immediately regained his interest. He wrote but a strategy for ministry, became enthusiastic and had new joy in serving the Lord.

Without a strategy, people don't know what to do. A pastor visited me one day from a nearby city. He was new, fresh out of seminary. He took the pastorate of a small church that had been struggling for several years. He proceeded to ask me some basic questions about what pastors should do. He said that he sat in his office day after day and nothing was happening. No one came by to see him. No one called him. He was bored and had nothing to do. Frankly, I had a hard time identifying with this young man! But I realized that he was serious, and he had no strategy. When I told him our strategy and gave him some ideas, he was overwhelmed. He didn't realize there was so much to do!

A common complaint in Christian organizations (that often goes unnoticed by the leadership) is that people don't know what to do. They have time on their hands. They don't know the overall strategy or how it applies to them in their area of ministry.

Without a strategy, we don't know how to get things accomplished. Strategy includes planning. Planning involves the "how" of organization. Things like personnel, resources, etc., tell us how to arrive at the goals we want to accomplish. Organizations that have no strategy make it difficult for the people who work for them to accomplish things.

In a large organization it seems like the channels through which you must go to accomplish something are endless. It has been my observation that a person can work for the organization for a considerable length of time and still not know how to get things done in the most efficient manner. A strategy should help. In that strategy, the process by which something is accomplished should be clearly outlined. The chain of command should be described so that the individual worker has no doubt as to how things can get done and through whom they must go for approval.

Having said all of that, experience reminds me that the process by which things are done needs to be upgraded constantly and brought before the people involved in the organization. Staff changes can affect the process. Equipment can easily break down. Supplies can run out. Schedules can be changed. All of this demands communication with workers. Reminders must come often as to how things can and should be done.

Without a strategy, we have no way to evaluate what we're doing. That may be the reason why so many leaders fail to have a strategy. We don't want to be evaluated by any form of measurement. It is too simple to spot weaknesses and failures in the organization. But, evaluation must go on. A leader's task is to evaluate constantly, cutting back on unproductive areas, and adding supplies and people to promising areas of growth.

I asked a pastor friend, "How are things going in your church?" He said, "I have no idea." He was honest, but after a few moments of discussion I learned he had no strategy. He did not know what his objectives were; he thus had no goals, or plans. No wonder he did not know how things were going in his own church!

The greatest danger in evaluation is when you compare your work with someone else. There is no need to do that. You set the strategy for your church, and stick with it! Don't worry about what the other person in another organization is doing! The question is, are you achieving the goals which you have set for your ministry? If you are, praise the Lord! That's what counts! God is not evaluating us on the basis of what someone else has done!

Without a strategy, we reveal a lack of commitment in the exercise of spiritual leadership. Talk is cheap. With our mouths we may profess to be committed to high and lofty purposes, but without a clearly-defined strategy, there's no real commitment to those purposes. A strategy suggests a certain seriousness about our spiritual leadership. We must know where we are going and how we are going to get there.

Musical chairs in the ministry is common. Pastors move quickly from one church to another, with each church suffering in the process. They are supposed to be spiritual leaders, but where are they going? A well-defined strategy will stop the constant changing of pastorates. It takes time to develop a strategy. Happy the Christian organization that has a strategy which demands a long term leadership.

One pastor friend saw that his constant moves from church to church was directly related to the lack of goals and objectives in his ministry. As soon as he wrote them down on paper, he caught a vision of a long term pastorate, and has settled down into a successful one at the present time.

Without a strategy, we will easily give up in a crisis. A strategy will help you to be patient when things take a turn for the worse. When that slump hits, your strategy can sustain you. There will be temporary setbacks along the way, but your strategy helps you to put them in proper perspective.

A pastor from a nearby city called one day to tell me he was quitting his ministry in that church. The church was in a period of decline and he wanted out before it was too late, whatever that meant. I encouraged him to stay. The words "I quit" ought to be removed from the spiritual leader's vocabulary. He failed to take my advice (happens a lot), but has lived to regret it. He feels now that he made a mistake. His problem? He had no strategy—no goals or objectives. It happens so often, you'd think leaders would respond and write out that strategy! However, human nature being what it is, many leaders continue to ignore this most basic fact of leadership—you must know where you are going if people are going to follow you!

How Much of Your Life Is Affected by Your Strategy?

Once you understand what a strategy is and why it is so important, every area of your life is included in your strategy. Actually, there are three basic areas affected by your strategy: your personal life, your family life, and your organizational life.

Personal objectives must be established and goals developed. A quick look at those personal goals will reveal many of the frustrations that a leader can feel. He can easily be frustrated in his life because he is not achieving any personal objectives and goals that he may have for himself.

For example, a leader may have a personal objective of keeping in excellent physical condition. He may set a goal of exercising twice a week. If his work schedule does not allow for this personal goal to be achieved he will become frustrated and in some cases the quality of his work can diminish.

To the believer, family goals are priorities. To spend time each week with your marital partner or your children is a must. It is most discouraging and damaging when these goals cannot be achieved. Leaders will do well to pay more attention to personal and family goals. They may discover roots of frustration and disappointment that presently affect their job.

Organizational goals must be established within the framework of priorities, especially as it relates to personal and family goals. A person's job is not more important than his family. But, achieving a balance between each of these areas—personal, family, and organizational—is not always easy.

During the first years of our marriage, my wife and I tried to establish the importance of our relationship by spending at least one evening together alone. We kept our date night faithfully. Later we changed to one day together (while the kids were in school). Every week we look forward to our one day together. It has helped us to establish the priority of one family goal we have—to stay best friends by being alone together at least one day a week. It's measurable, so it's a goal. The objective is to be best friends. Adjustments have to be made from time to time, but they are few and far between.

The reason why this is important to me (my family

goal to be with my wife one day a week) is because of what I know the Bible teaches about marriage, my personal need for companionship and love, and also the effect upon my job. I work better and more efficiently when I have time alone with my wife. When things are right between us, my work becomes much more enjoyable.

Why Is the Setting of Goals So Important?

It is impossible to determine the effectiveness of your life if you don't set goals. It is my opinion that everyone has goals. They may not write them down or even be able to communicate them to others, but they have them just the same. If you could penetrate a person's inner feelings and discover his goals, you could tell much about that person and his chances for productivity.

Sometimes the goals we set are unrealistic. They do not carefully evaluate the potential of people and resources. For example, it is unrealistic for a church in a community of 10,000 people isolated by 100 miles from any other community, to set a goal of 20,000 people as members of that church! It may not be unrealistic to set a goal like that in a major metropolitan area.

On the other hand, the goals we have may not be attainable because they are not specific. A goal to reach as many people as possible with the gospel of Christ is really not a goal, but a fine purpose or objective. A specific goal within that objective might be to share the gospel door to door with 10,000 homes in your community in a three-month period of time.

Some do not like goals at all. What about the sovereignty of God? Well, God is sovereign all right, and He is running things in this universe. However, He does it through people. He ordains the means as well as the end. We are responsible to Him. Goals often reflect our con-

139

fidence and faith in a sovereign God. Do we trust Him to perform His work in us?

The so-called "numbers game" is where the problem of goals is usually fought. To have a bigger attendance this week than last week is a goal, but it might be unworthy of believers committed to biblical principles. Our goals are sometimes based on a carnal motive of comparison with others. The only One to whom we are accountable is God. Contests, prizes, competition, and awards are often used to stimulate people toward the achieving of certain goals. Without getting into an argument over the validity of such methods in Christian organizations, we can at least emphasize the underlying motive of such methods. If the methods do not violate God's Word and if the motive is worthy and biblical, then the use of the methods must be allowable. You may not want to use any of those methods, but for some, they may be permissible.

Learn this truth: It is unwise to develop goals based upon comparison with others. Don't try to do something bigger just to be bigger than someone else. Be what God wants you to be. You are responsible to Him for the use of your talents and abilities, not for what someone else has.

Some leaders trying to avoid the use of numbers wind up doing nothing. They have no specific goals and thus no way to evaluate their work. They never try to improve themselves or their organization. They will watch a situation deteriorate before doing anything about it. Such apathy and laziness is not a characteristic of the spiritual leader. There is always room for improvement. The Lord deserves our very best!

It has been my experience that numbers are vital to proper evaluation. Consider the Sunday School class that continues to decline in attendance over an extended period of time. An evaluation must be made. It would never be made had not the numbers been evident, showing the decline. The reason for the decline is another subject that takes careful evaluation and consideration of all the facts. Leaders who do not care what happens and do nothing to change things are only revealing that they are not worthy to be leaders.

Good leaders do have a strategy. It is essential, not optional. In one sense, we all have a strategy whether written or not, whether good or bad. The strategy of some is mediocrity. They simply do nothing but try to maintain the status quo, an impossible attempt.

The next chapter considers how to develop and use your strategy. If you are presently serving as a spiritual leader, why not take a break from reading, and start writing down your strategy? Don't forget to set goals in your personal life and family life, as well as your organizational life.

Leader's Checklist

1. What are your objectives? List three major ones.
2. Write your own definition of an objective and a goal.
3. Do you have a philosophy of ministry? Does it include the five things mentioned in the beginning of this chapter?
4. Do you have a strategy for your personal life? Your family life? Your organizational life? Describe these strategies in one or two paragraphs each.
5. Are you able to set realistic goals? Specific goals? Name some of your goals for the year, the month, the week.
6. Does competition or adversity cause you to set more goals and try harder to reach them? Can you think of a recent example?

HOW TO DEVELOP A GOOD STRATEGY— AND USE IT

The basic purpose of a good strategy is, of course, to give glory to God (see 1 Cor. 10:31) in all we do. The leader will also be committed to doing his best in everything, and influencing the greatest amount of people he possibly can for the cause of Jesus Christ.

A good strategy flows out of a life lived for the glory of God. If the leader's purpose in life is to have the largest church in the world, or become the most famous speaker of all time, etc., then his strategy will reflect these selfish motives, and not the glory of God.

What Objectives Should a Spiritual Leader Have?

A good strategy is composed of objectives, goals, priorities, planning, and guidelines. Every leader will be different in designing his strategy than other leaders. However, the spiritual leader will usually come up with similar objectives to other spiritual leaders. Objectives are the basic purposes of the organization.

Our church has three basic objectives that control what we do and teach: evangelism, edification, and expansion. The definitions of each of those objectives is so very important. Not every one will agree on the definitions we use, but that really is not important to our discussion. The important thing is to make sure when you write out your objectives that you give clear definitions so people know exactly what your organization's purposes are. It tells you much about that organization.

In our case, *evangelism* is the proclamation of the gospel to nonbelievers, resulting in their conversion to Jesus Christ, baptism in water, and membership in the local body of believers.

Some strategies of local churches design the objective of evangelism as being the sharing of the gospel to the nonbelieving world. That is good. But, it doesn't go far enough in our opinion, and the rest of the strategy is affected. The goals of the organization are the specific ways in which the objectives will be measured and accomplished. How can you design specific goals that are measurable in the area of baptism or church membership if they are not a part of your objective? Church growth is deeply affected by this point.

A conversation with a pastor in our area convinced me of the importance of baptism and church membership as a part of the basic objective of evangelism. (I was already convinced from Acts 2:41!) He and his church were quite committed to sharing the gospel with nonbelievers, and they had experienced many conversions to Christ. In fact, if all the people they had won to Christ had become responsible members of his church, that church would be the largest on the West Coast! As it was, it was a church of moderate size that had not grown numerically in several years. After talking with him about this, I realized the problem. They were not concerned about baptism and church membership in their view of evangelism. The strategy they had was fine in one area, but very deficient in others.

Whatever your objectives, make sure they state the

143

basic purposes of your organization in enough detail so that people know how to design goals that can be measured and accomplished. Spiritual leaders who want to do everything to the glory of God should also make sure that the objectives are based upon the Word of God (write in the Scripture references for people to study).

How to Design Specific Goals for Your Ministry

Goals are the specific ways in which the purposes of your organization will be measured and accomplished. According to most leaders I have talked with, writing specific goals is the problem. Very few do it. Goals should be written out frequently. They can change. Objectives remain the same.

In order to design specific goals for your ministry, a few basic points should be kept in mind.

Goals should be written for your personal life, family life, and organizational life. Your personal goals might involve recreation and exercise for health reasons, the writing of books, or the reading of books, traveling to various parts of the world, attending special seminars and conferences, etc. These personal goals will affect your organizational goals but they are not the same. Personal goals deal with the growth of the leader himself. Organizational goals deal with the organization's growth. The leader needs to grow regardless of the organization he is involved with.

Family goals, like vacations, sports/games, house, cars, investments, financial security, etc., are often affected by the organizational goals. The matter of priorities will often determine which takes precedent over the other. The leader's family is more important than the organization, but the way that importance is emphasized or determined is not an easy matter!

Once you can see on paper the specific goals you have

144

in each area you are in better position to evaluate the possibility of accomplishing these goals. You can see immediately where overlapping and conflict exist.

Goals should be written for the immediate as well as the long-range future. Long-range goals teach patience. They help you stick to the task in the midst of temporary setbacks. They encourage a longer ministry in one job and place. They give direction to the immediate goals. Immediate goals should be designed in an effort to accomplish long-range goals. Long-range goals can be based on any length of time within a person's lifetime.

It has been my experience that long-range goals that exceed 10 years in length are normally changed. So, a long-range goal to me is one that covers a 10-year period of time. At the end of the 10 years, write out goals for the next 10 years, and so on.

Long-range goals of 10 years in length should include some 5-year goals as well. This gives you a point for evaluation in achieving the 10-year goals. Evaluate the first 5 years on the basis of whether that experience will produce the 10-year goals. If not, then change what you are doing!

Immediate goals can be based on the day, week, month, or year. Perhaps all of those should be used. There are specific goals that I have in mind for each day. I like to write them down. There are immediate goals for this coming week that I must accomplish. In our ministry, our leaders must evaluate what we are doing every three months. We have what we call a quarterly planning session. We meet all day in an isolated place. Ideas are freely shared and goals determined, changed, or dropped.

Churches should establish specific goals for their ministries at least every year. The best time to do this is early summer. Plan the church year as though it begins in September. There are four basic patterns in the ministry of every church upon which you can base your planning: the first runs from after Labor Day until Christmas; the second pattern runs from after New Year's Day until Easter week; the third pattern runs from after Easter week until school is out; the fourth pattern is the summer, basically, July and August. Learn to plan and write specific goals for those four periods of time. Try not to overlap what you are doing into another pattern. Each summer you should re-evaluate your goals. Did you achieve them? What could you do differently or better?

Goals should have deadlines for accomplishing them. A common fallacy in thinking is that we can work on a particular matter at another time. There is no deadline, no time limit. As a result, the matter is usually put off until someone demands it be done by a certain time. Set deadlines for your goals. When is a project to be completed? Most leaders find that they are more productive when they have deadlines.

We publish a church newsletter. We learned that a deadline had to be set for the submission of articles for that newsletter. If the article was not submitted on time, it would have to wait for the next issue. No exceptions! It has a way of making everyone set goals and plan ahead!

As soon as the time limit for the accomplishing of your goals is over, immediately evaluate your goals. Do you need to establish other goals based on what you just did? Did you achieve your goals on time? Do you need to set another time limit?

Goals should be realistic based on time, resources, and personnel available. Be careful about this. It is better to achieve the goals, than to be impressed with the size of them but never achieve them! People will get discouraged if they can never achieve the goals which the spiritual leadership designs. Once several goals are achieved, then the faith and vision of the people can be stretched a little more. Set goals that will encourage the people and be realistic for them to accomplish.

If it normally takes two years to build a building the size you want, then don't set a goal of six months! Use your head! Set goals realistically.

One of the goals we set for our church one summer was to visit 17,000 homes in our immediate community, introducing ourselves, our ministry as a church, and our Lord Jesus Christ. We set the goal deadline. It was to be accomplished in eight weeks by people going out one night a week for about one hour of visiting. Over 200 people participated. The goal was reachable because we had spent time in evaluating the number of homes, the time in which to do it, and the personnel available to do the work. It was a realistic goal for us.

Goals should be directly related to one of the basic objectives of the organization. Setting a goal just to have a goal is not good strategy. People will get tired of that. It ought to be simple to read a goal and immediately know what objective it is related to. If the objective is not the purpose of the goal, then the goal will detract from the effectiveness of the organization. It will drain off manpower, money, and time. The organization cannot stand many of these additional— beyond the objectives—goals. They are growth-restricting obstacles whether they are recognized as such or not.

If the objective is evangelism in a given organization. but one of the goals is to take people to Israel to study archaeology, that organization will be weakened by the goal. The goal does not accomplish the objective. Leaders should learn to avoid goals that take people away from the main objectives of the organization.

Goals should be communicated well in advance of the time period planned for accomplishing them. Many mistakes are made in this area. A few leaders establish goals and then announce them to the people who are to be involved in accomplishing the goals the week before the project or task begins! It's not enough time. People need to be prepared mentally for what is expected of them.

In our church, it has been our experience that goals affecting the entire church must be planned and communicated at least six months in advance. The two months before a certain project, task, or ministry begins is the most crucial time of communication. All parties involved must have time to prepare for the project. There must be sufficient time for promoting the project —one week a public announcement, another week a mailing, another week a sign, another week a skit, another week a brochure, etc. Goals must be continually communicated. Don't pull any surprises on your people and then complain when the response is not good and the goal is not accomplished!

How Do You Know What the Priorities Are?

In any effective strategy, leaders must establish priorities. Priorities are the factors that determine when and why things are done. When you have a great deal of goals, you must decide which ones are most important for you to work on today, and in what order.

Sometimes a leader has too many goals he is trying to accomplish. That's another reason why we need to establish priorities. Some leaders who are "workaholics" have a tendency to design too many goals for themselves and other employees. They will drive themselves and others until someone has a breakdown! Rome wasn't built in a day, and you'll be much happier if you don't try!

One simple way to establish priorities among all the goals that people want to accomplish is by putting a value system on the goals. Have a category called "most important," then "somewhat important," and then "not quite so important," and of course, "not important at all!"

In dealing with priorities you must establish the time involved to do it. Here is where many leaders fail. Some people like to spell priority t-i-m-e! If I tell my wife that she is a priority in my life but I spend no time alone with her, she should begin to wonder about my claim!

The first thing is to set a deadline for completing a given goal. Next, you must estimate the time needed to accomplish this goal by the desired deadline. Then, you must plan segments of time into your weekly calendar that will meet the demands of that goal. If it is not important to you (matter of priorities), you probably won't spend time on it!

Let's try to illustrate the matter of priorities by picturing a leader working at his desk in his office. His secretary calls him on the phone and gives him this message: "Your wife is on the phone." Some leaders will immediately take the call, especially when the wife is not known to abuse the privilege, because it is a priority to them. Suppose the secretary calls and says, "Your wife called and said to pick up your suit at the cleaners." Immediately, you must evaluate the importance of that call and the time needed to act upon it. If you don't need the suit for a few days, it would seem ridiculous to get up immediately and go to the cleaners for the suit.

Sometimes, there are emergencies that must be handled and these have a way of demonstrating priorities. Suppose the secretary called and said, "Leave your office; the building is on fire!" It shouldn't take you too long to respond! We all need to learn the lesson of time.

Priorities will determine when you do something and for how long you must do it.

In order for priorities to function properly a leader must discern the difference between that which must be done today and that which, although extremely important, could wait until tomorrow. Learn to do the "must" things first. Your mental attitude and response will be much more relaxed when facing other priorities. Some priorities should be fixed in given time slots each week. There are certain things that should be done at the same time every week. If one of your priorities is to spend one day a week with your wife alone, then schedule it! Whenever you have the opportunity to do something else on that day, you must ask the question, "Is it a higher priority than my wife?"

Priorities are built primarily upon your commitment. What you believe is important comes from what you have committed yourself to do or be. The spiritual leader must begin with his personal commitment to the Lord. That is best understood in a time of private prayer and study of the Word. If it is the priority you say it is, then schedule a time each day for it and keep your appointments! A spiritual leader must also be committed to his wife and family. Again, schedule those times, and keep your promises! A leader must also have a commitment to other members of the Body of Christ. What time do you give to this each week? We must also be committed to the world around us. Again, what time is given for this? Our commitment to the work of Christ must also be scheduled. If, as a spiritual leader, you work full-time as a salaried employee in the Lord's work, then the time you give is fairly well structured for you. But if you are not full-time, then you must decide how much time you can give to the Lord's work. Time often tells us what the real priorities of our life are.

One final thing before we leave the subject of priorities. Many leaders do not carefully evaluate the importance of time given to protect one's health. This involves our diet, rest, exercise, and relaxation. Leaders feel the pressure of achievement and being an example to others. Leaders do not want to have others accuse them of laziness or lack of desire to work. They often feel embarrassed about taking time off, or spending time each week in physical exercise and recreation. There are, of course, many who abuse this need and spend too much time at it and thus neglect more important things. However, the facts show that the real problem among most aggressive leader-types is the failure to schedule time for rest, relaxation, and recreation.

It is easy to prove the fallacy of this kind of thinking that keeps working to achieve goals without taking time off from work. Longevity is greatly reduced, humanly speaking, when we do not have proper rest, diet, and exercise. Heart attacks are frequent among leaders (often at an early age). Leaders have a tendency or responsibility to sit at a desk during the day. They do not move around as they should. They ride in cars when they should walk and take elevators when they should walk the stairs. We learn to enjoy the luxuries of life, and forget about our physical condition.

Many Christian organizations will do well to check up on their leaders in this particular area. More can be accomplished in 30 years than in 10, even at a slower pace! Your health is a priority to you right now. The effectiveness of leaders in their present work is affected by the kind of diet, rest, and recreation that they have.

What Do We Mean by Planning?

Good strategies are based on careful planning. Planning is the process by which we seek ways to achieve our goals. Planning takes time as well as foresight. We must constantly anticipate and think ahead. That for which we plan may have no existence outside our own minds, but it is a vital part of strategy. Sometimes your plans do not materialize. When this happens, it is no time for discouragement, but rather an opportunity to see God work things out for His glory in spite of your unfulfilled plans.

Proverbs 15:22 says, "Without consultation, plans are frustrated, but with many counselors they succeed." It takes time to plan. There are many details to be worked out and problems to solve. Talking with others about it is important to the success of your plans. If you have five minutes to achieve a goal, spend two of those minutes planning.

Some leaders think that planning is the opposite of trusting God. That kind of thinking is similar to the preacher who believes that he doesn't need to study because he wants to be led of the Holy Spirit while preaching! Obviously, God can lead and direct us in our planning! We must depend upon His guidance at that point as well as in the actual ministry for which we are planning.

There are four essential ingredients to good planning:

Personnel. Describing who is involved and who is responsible, and who will do the work is vital to good planning. The name of the game here is communication. The leader starts the process in his own mind, and begins by considering which personnel are in the chain of command and responsibility. Include them first in your planning.

Next, begin to communicate with others who will be affected by the planning and include their ideas and suggestions. Determine which personnel will be responsible for what areas of the plan. Make assignments with deadlines. Make sure the personnel involved in the planning know who to report to when their work is done.

In my early ministry I thought that the fewest possible should do the planning. There are still times when that must be done. But, experience has shown me that the more people involved in the planning process, the greater measure of success. Take it in stages, and decide when to include others, but seek to include as many as possible at the right times. This often takes the wisdom of Solomon!

Resources. The most important resource we have is the ministry of the Holy Spirit in the lives of people. These are not the personnel who do the planning, but the people who will carry out the project—who actually do the work. Materials can be replaced or discarded, but people cannot. God works through people!

In addition to the people, you must evaluate in your planning what materials will be needed to carry out the project or goal. Will it be a brochure, or a letter? Will it be a sign, or sound equipment? Will it be tables and chairs or a room to rent? These and many more questions like them will have to be pursued.

There is also the matter of finances. Very few projects can be accomplished without the expenditure of money. Good planning pays much attention to cost. Leaders who do not evaluate such matters will soon lose the support of those around them. It is easy in most cases to determine how much a project will cost. The problem comes when deciding how to raise the money that will be needed. Where the money comes from is a vital question to good planning.

Obstacles. Failure to plan for obstacles almost insures that they will come! Good planning must anticipate problems that can develop. It must also discuss how to overcome obstacles whether they be financial or merely the opinions of people. Overcoming obstacles is not what every person likes to do, but it is necessary and it seems to be a quality of leadership.

The late Dr. Bob Jones, Sr. had a saying like this: "The test of your character is what it takes to stop you!" How true that is! Many give up too easily. The obstacles, problems, or difficulties seem too great to overcome so the project is abandoned. But wait a minute! Was it a worthwhile goal? Will it meet a real need? Will it give glory to God? Is it based on biblical authority? Is it the will of God? Obstacles are there as tests to our faith, as well as sometimes indicating a closed door.

When anyone says, "'It can't be done," it makes men of faith hurt inside. They feel that God has been questioned. Jesus said, "With men it is impossible, but not with God; for all things are possible with God" (Mark 10:27). When facing obstacles, it is good to look at the alternatives you have.

• The door is closed; go no farther in pursuing your goal.

• There is something we have overlooked which is being brought to our attention by the obstacle we face.

• Our faith needs to be tested.

• The obstacle will increase our dedication and commitment.

• There is another way of doing it.

• We are being reminded of our limitations; it causes us to depend more upon God.

Don't be afraid of obstacles, they can turn out to be great blessings in disguise! Learn to plan for them and prepare to face them.

Evaluation. The failure to evaluate goals both before and after they are achieved is a serious mistake. No planning can be really effective that does not take evaluation seriously. The best time to evaluate is immediately

when a goal is achieved or when it has failed. Ask many questions with the word "why" in them. For example:
- Why did so few young people attend that occasion?
- Why did we fail to communicate to our adults?
- Why did the expense exceed the budget we set?
- Why did the people feel we had not considered their needs and feelings in the matter?
- Why was the sound equipment not effective?

Put your evaluation on paper and file it in a place to which you will turn often for help and advice. If some particular idea failed miserably, then write down the reasons why and file it for future protection. After all, you don't want to make the same mistake twice.

In all this discussion concerning planning, remember that it also takes time. Is there time in your schedule for planning? If not, why not? Could it be because there are no specific goals governing your life? Leaders really have no choice, they must plan or they better plan to fail. The most important planning time for the leader is the time he spends alone. Do not begin to plan with others until you have had time to plan and think on the project or goals involved. You must be mentally prepared when taking time to plan with others.

Why Do We Need Guidelines?

Without guidelines our plans will often fail or, at best, lose their ring of authority and urgency. Guidelines should be established that will cover different situations and various kinds of goals. They must allow for flexibility and change but they must also be enforced and applied. If you cannot enforce your guidelines, you might have the wrong set of guidelines or you yourself are lacking in good leadership. The subject of guidelines is very much related to a previous chapter on authority. Morality is in the background, and without a standard of morality it is almost impossible to establish guidelines. The spiritual leader bases his guidelines upon the morality of the Scriptures.

Guidelines are the moral and ethical framework in which the organization will seek to accomplish its goals. Without them, the organization loses the perspective of its original objectives and often uses methods that cause the eventual decline of that organization. Guidelines keep us on the right track and faithful to our original commitments.

Here are a few guidelines that illustrate what they are and how they affect the Christian organization:

Nothing shall be done which violates a principle of God's Word. In our staff meetings, a discussion which brings up a matter that is in violation of God's Word immediately ends. We cannot do it.

Emphasis shall be upon people rather than upon tasks to be done. One of our objectives in our church is edification which involves the building up of people to maturity in Christ. It is more important to build the person, than to use the person to build the work.

All ministries and activities should be evaluated in the light of our objectives. This is simply a reminder to all of us to stick to the objectives. It is relatively easy to develop goals that have nothing to do with our objectives.

Methods of training shall concentrate on the discipleship of the few to reach the many, and this to be done by mature believers. Our experience has proven the importance of this guideline. Using people in leadership roles who are not mature hinders the accomplishment of our objectives. Trying to motivate the masses of people is not nearly as successful as motivating the few to reach the many.

All positions of leadership and service to be based upon

a godly life-style. Enough said. Breakdowns in strategies are often found at this point!

A person's gifts, abilities, or talents will be confirmed by others in this body of believers before being placed into leadership. We all think better of ourselves than we actually are. We need the evaluations of other people before we place people into leadership.

The list of guidelines could be expanded. It simply reveals the moral and ethical framework in which we seek to accomplish our goals. The guidelines are vital to the matter of spiritual commitment.

A good strategy is composed of five things:

- *Objectives*—the basic purposes of the organization.
- *Goals*—the specific ways in which the purposes of the organization will be measured and accomplished.
- *Priorities*—the factors that determine when and why things are done.
- *Planning*—the process used to achieve the goals (includes personnel, resources, obstacles, and evaluation).
- *Guidelines*—the moral and ethical framework in which the organization will seek to accomplish its goals.

Leader's Checklist

1. What are your organization's objectives? Do you have a clear definition for each of these?
2. How frequently do you write out your goals for your personal life? Family life? Organizational life?
3. Do you have immediate as well as long-range goals?
4. Have you prioritized your goals?
5. Does your planning include the "four essentials"?
6. Do you have guidelines for establishing your objectives? Are they written down?

PART VII

LOVE:
DO YOU CARE
FOR THE PEOPLE
AROUND YOU?

IT'S NOT EASY TO LOVE PEOPLE

The badge of discipleship is love for one another (see John 13:34,35). It is impossible to deal with spiritual leadership and not talk about loving people. Management books from the secular world may leave it out of the discussion, but Christians cannot.

Loving people is not as simple as it sounds! Leaders know that, but they don't often know why. Some of us give up too easily in the attempt to show love. One of our staff members has a discipleship group that meets early in the morning before the men go off to work. One day, one of the members of that group failed to show up for the Bible study. The other members decided to go to his house, wake him up, and have the Bible study right there! They didn't want him to miss out, and they loved him enough to do something about it. I don't think he'll miss one of the meetings again.

In the secular world, leaders are sometimes separated from those working under them. Different privileges and facilities are given to the leaders, separating them from the workers. Close friendships are not cultivated between leaders and workers. They are considered to be dangerous. Leaders stay aloof from the workers. All of this reveals a failure to understand the importance of love between leader and worker.

There are certain burdens and responsibilities that only the leader can bear. He cannot share some things with the workers even though he might want to do so. But staying completely away from the people under him is a great mistake. It is a dangerous principle to isolate yourself from those with whom you work. When Jesus called His disciples according to Mark 3:14, it was "that they might be *with Him.*" Close association between the leader and the ones under that leadership is vital to effective spiritual leadership. There must be a sense of unity, fellowship, partnership and most of all, love. Those under a spiritual leadership must know that the leader loves them and works for them.

But, let's face it, it's not easy to love certain people! God, of course, knows that problem in our lives and has provided resources for us to draw upon that will give us a love for people regardless of how unlovable they might be. Loving people does not mean being dishonest or deceitful. The arena of God's love is very practical and open for all to examine. It's a combination of little things that we do for people.

When God's love is controlling, you don't have to fake it or put on a false front. You can be real, honest, and transparent before others. You can relax and enjoy your relationships with people and not be worrying about what others think of you. For leaders, this is a special problem because they are very much aware of what others think and say of them. They are always out front for everyone to see and evaluate. Their lives are more exposed to others than most people ever experience. They must work with all types of personalities, and they do not enjoy the luxury of non-leaders who can easily walk away from a relationship because they have no responsibility.

Leadership Problems in Loving People

Before we take an in-depth look at God's love which all leaders must understand and apply in their relationships with people, we need to identify the common problems which leaders have in showing love for people. Leaders will identify easily with these problems and all prospective leaders must learn to recognize them and know how to deal with them.

Some leaders are too busy. A leader or administrator is by nature more goal-oriented than most people. The leader seeks to accomplish things and achieve as much as possible. Frequently, this causes the leader to appear, and maybe become, insensitive to people. Often the leader feels pressured by the multitude of his responsibilities and simply does not have time to spend with people with whom he works. It often becomes a matter of priorities.

To the leader, the task to be achieved seems more important than any one individual's needs or problems. There is a sense in which that is true. But it is also dangerous when people are ignored or neglected. Jesus had time for people, the individual as well as the crowd. Leaders must arrange their priorities so that time spent with people is not looked upon as time wasted or time that is not important.

It is possible to be too available to people and thus hinder the effectiveness of your leadership and the needs of others who depend upon the leader fulfilling his or her responsibilities. However, there must be some time when the leader shows the ones he works with that they are more important to him than the tasks or the projects that need to be done. If this is not done, the

162

leader will discover that the very leadership he needs to accomplish those important tasks has diminished and is not there when he needs it. Love and loyalty are very closely related. The more love demonstrated between the leader and the people he leads, the stronger the ties and loyalties.

There are too many demands upon himself. The worst problem the leader has is himself. The leader is often more of a perfectionist than the average person. He expects things to be done right and with a certain class that speaks well of the organization or of the work he is doing. He pressures and drives himself in areas that others could handle. It is more difficult to let go than it is to take on more work. He thrives on work and normally enjoys it. The problem that develops is rarely recognized by the leader at the time it is happening. The demands and pressures he puts upon his own life and schedule make it virtually impossible for him to have time for loving people. He justifies this by reasoning that people will appreciate the hours of hard work that he engages in, and will readily see his true motives that they are good and beneficial in the long run for all concerned.

However, people need love and they need to know that the leader loves them. And, frankly, that takes time! A worker may need the love and encouragement of the leader, but because of the pressure and demands upon the leader, which the leader often places upon himself, that person feels guilty for taking the valuable time of the leader. The leader must be more relaxed and allow time for others. In a sense, he or she must become more disciplined in the use of time. Leaders must learn to allow time for showing love to others as surely as programming time for other things.

Leaders must also learn to relax more and to ease the

pressure a little. They'll probably live longer if they do! Look over your schedule and responsibilities. Are there things that others could do that you are presently doing? What things could you eliminate that you do now if you were required to do so? What causes you the most pressure and frustration? How important is it that you continue doing what you are currently doing? These questions and many more must be continually asked by the leader.

Some leaders are too impatient with the people around them. There are many reasons why leaders are impatient with those with whom they work. Regardless of the reasons, impatience does not belong in the life-style of the spiritual leader. It is the opposite of a Spirit-filled life. People around such a leader see him or her as unloving and uncaring.

Impatience is reflected in the way we talk or look. There are the extremes of those who talk louder or more rapidly because they are impatient or continually look (or hit) at their watches while someone is talking to them. More subtle manifestations of impatience are seen when the leader fails to delegate responsibility to others or does something that someone under him was supposed to do but hasn't done it as yet.

Sometimes what appears to be impatience to some is wisdom and good leadership to others. When someone sits in your office and continually wastes time with idle and meaningless chatter, manifesting laziness and an undisciplined life, it is not impatience on the part of the leader that cuts off such practice and forces the person to go back to work—that is a part of good leadership! Leaders need wisdom at times to know the difference between what is impatience on their part and what is good and disciplined leadership.

Impatience often develops over the speed at which

others do their work. It is important that leaders do not make demands upon people that are greater than their capabilities. Sometimes a leader will expect the person under him to perform at a rate or level which the leader alone can do. This will, of course, reflect a lack of love on the part of the leader.

At times it may be a problem of discipline. Some people are lazy and procrastinate. If the leader is loving, he will take into consideration the abilities and talents of those under him, and seek to challenge without overwhelming the person. The leader will give enough time for that person to complete the task assigned without pressure that the leader would place upon himself but which others cannot stand. A loving leader will do all he can to protect those under him from failing. He will be patient with them and find joy in watching them grow and overcome what may have been a weakness in the past.

Some are too insecure about their own position of leadership. Many leaders feel threatened. Sometimes they are threatened by bright and promising people within the organization who appear to have talents and abilities that the leader does not possess. Sometimes their insecurity comes from the lack of appreciation or acceptance. If people do not give some positive feedback to the leader from time to time, he will have a tendency to doubt and question his effectiveness and, as a result, feel threatened. Leaders have problems with job security. This is a special problem among pastoral leaders. The average church cannot claim long pastorates in its history. Often it seems like musical chairs are being played as pastors frequently change churches in order to get a fresh start or to run away from a previous problem. A lack of success in one church can hinder a man's future in another.

Whatever the causes behind the insecurity a leader might feel, the result of this is usually a lack of love toward others. People who are insecure in their personalities, abilities, or occupation have a tendency to cover up in public and hide behind past achievements. A close relationship with another person in the organization may appear to be a dangerous thing. The leader may fear what that person will do one day with what has been shared in intimate friendship. God's love is, of course, much different! But leaders are aware that human standards of love and human weaknesses can often get in the way of God's love. The results can be very threatening to the leader!

One of the most obvious symptoms of an insecure leader is a judgmental attitude toward others, especially those who represent spiritual leadership. A critical spirit flows from such a leader and derogatory remarks are common. The leader tries by the criticism of others to strengthen his own position or authority in the eyes of others. It usually backfires!

Leaders may be too sensitive about what other people think. It is easy to ignore a loving response to another person on the basis of what others might think. Some pastors feel that to share a word of encouragement to one member and not to all the members is wrong. It might lead the others to think that the pastor doesn't really care about them or that he favors one member above the others. But the real issue is not what others think, but what does God want us to do? Was there a real need for it? To have a group-consciousness where you only express love in public meetings and ignore the personal times when you should be "individual-conscious" is a great mistake. The result of such action will be a leader who seems hypocritical—loving in public but not in private! When a pastor is out of the pulpit people

166

must know that he is loving and kind. The pastor's relationship to individuals during the week is what enhances his pulpit ministry on Sunday.

Spiritual leaders must be careful about evaluating their actions in the light of what others will think or say. The One to whom we are accountable is God Himself. When we are right with Him, it matters not what others think! That moment of sharing the love of Christ with another person will become the strength of your ministry. There will always be people who will criticize you. Be careful about being too sensitive. In some things our skin must be as tough as the hippopotamus!

Leaders may be too afraid of close relationships. Some leaders believe that close relationships and leadership are incompatible. This is unfortunate. It leads to a leadership without love, which in the final analysis is not spiritual leadership. Leaders often build around themselves certain walls of protection that do not allow other individuals to get close to them. Close relationships with others will expose the leader for what he or she really is. Your faults and weaknesses become evident to the other person, and some leaders feel that when that happens they lose a certain prestige or respect in the eyes of others. You never know what that person might do with what he knows.

There is also a tendency to believe that people will not like you as much once they learn about your faults. But, Proverbs 17:17 reminds us that "A friend loves at all times, and a brother is born for adversity." In verse 9 of that same chapter it says, "He who covers a transgression seeks love, but he who repeats a matter separates intimate friends."

Every leader needs that close friendship, someone who knows what he is like and still loves him and protects him. The close friend is also the one to rebuke the leader. Proverbs 27:6 says, "Faithful are the wounds of a friend, but deceitful are the kisses of an enemy." A close friend will help the leader to have a proper perspective about situations and a clearer understanding about his own motives. Proverbs 27:17 speaks to this when it says, "Iron sharpens iron, so one man sharpens another."

Most people will never have many close friends. Acquaintances and social friendships can be many, but the circle of intimate or close friends is very small. That kind of friendship is developed over a long period of time and tested in many different situations. It is dangerous to share too many personal things with people who are not close friends. It takes time to build such a friendship and to have a mutual trust and love that protects and defends.

It is in the arena of close friendship that a leader learns to love. When a leader isolates himself from others to the extent that he or she has no close friends, the leader's ability to grow in love is greatly reduced.

Learning to Love People

Learning to love people is essential to spiritual leadership. In order to overcome some of the leadership problems just mentioned, a few basic principles will be needed.

Consistency. Learn to show love to everyone and at all times. A loving leader can be counted on in times of difficulty and trial. His love is always there.

A dear friend was trying to cut down a huge tree in his front yard. A tremendous storm was in progress which was uprooting many trees. He needed help. He called me and told me his predicament and emphasized the urgency of it. I immediately rushed over to his house and helped him. It was a good thing; that tree almost

168

crashed into the house! We were soaking wet and he turned to me and said, "Thanks, friend!" That was worth it all!

Need. If leaders are showing love, they are inevitably attracted by the needs of others. They're willing to help. First John 3:17 says, "But whoever has the world's goods, and beholds his brother in need and closes his heart against him, how does the love of God abide in him?"

One of our staff members is of great encouragement to me. Whenever I have a need, he's there. I know he loves me. I needed a car and, without another thought, he gave me his to drive as long as I wanted. He responds to needs.

Trust. A leader can destroy his effectiveness if he cannot be trusted. Can the reputation of another co-worker be placed safely in your hands when that person is absent? More friendships are destroyed through gossip than possibly anything else. Proverbs 11:13 says, "He who goes about as a talebearer reveals secrets, but he who is trustworthy conceals a matter."

Leaders must never betray confidences. Things that are shared with you in private should stay that way— private!

We were discussing a certain person in a staff meeting as to whether he would make a good leader in a certain area of ministry. The one thing against him was that he could not be trusted. He had a problem with gossip. He could not keep confidences. We decided not to place him into leadership at that time.

Self-control. Because it's not so easy to love certain people, we sometimes lose control. Leaders who fly off the handle or are always blowing off about things are demonstrating a lack of love for those around them. Self-control is a fruit of the Holy Spirit (see Gal. 5:22,

23), and is a must in the life of the spiritual leader. The contrast between a person who has little except love, and a person who has much but doesn't love, is graphically illustrated in Proverbs 15:16-18. A situation without love according to that passage is one where there is anger and strife.

People who work with leaders who lack self-control come to believe that they do not love them. It's a rather obvious conclusion.

Sincerity. It's the opposite of being hypocritical. The word was used in ancient times for an actor who played another role by simply putting on a mask. We get our word "hypocrite" from this idea of putting on a mask. One who is sincere refuses to play the other role. He is unhypocritical. Love must be sincere and from the heart. You cannot fake it!

Many leadership problems could be resolved if leaders loved with sincerity and truth. Deception and dishonesty will destroy spiritual leadership. They will undermine people's confidence in you, and cause them to question the level of your commitment and love.

Forgiveness. Ephesians 4:32 tells us to be kind to one another, forgiving each other. First Peter 4:8 says that fervent love will cover a multitude of sins. Without forgiveness, leaders cannot show love. People respond to those who are forgiving and seeking to restore and rebuild relationships rather than tearing them down.

If leaders cannot forgive others for what they have said or done, the people around them will sense this bitter, unforgiving spirit, and will withdraw from close identification and support of that leader.

One lady shared with me why she was not supportive of a certain staff member. She observed his lack of forgiveness toward another lady, and did not want to experience the same kind of thing. She withdrew from

170

that staff member's area of ministry because of it. I encouraged her to be forgiving, but I also went to the staff member and shared the importance of his forgiving the other lady. He responded well, and both ladies are now part of his ministry!

Leaders have problems loving people just like everyone else. It is easy to forget the value of love in human relationships. Song of Solomon 8:6,7 tells us that love is strong as death, and that many waters cannot quench it, nor rivers overflow it. All the talents and abilities in the world cannot substitute for love. Leaders must put the emphasis upon it that God does. Love alone can withstand all the pressures of life and endure all the problems of people.

Leader's Checklist

1. Do you find some people in your work or ministry who are hard to love? Who are they? How are you handling them?

2. Do you feel that you are "too busy" to show love to people around you?

3. If you have too many demands upon you, are there things others could do that you are presently doing to relieve you of some of the burdens? List some of those.

4. Are you patient with co-workers and others with whom you associate? Do you know what causes your impatience?

5. Can you name some symptoms of insecurity in your own life?

6. Have there been times when you were overly sensitive to what someone said? How did you overcome this?

7. Do you take time to build close relationships with other people? How?

8. Of the six basic principles of learning to love other people, which ones do you need to work on in your life?

HOW TO LOVE PEOPLE WITH GOD'S LOVE!

The real answer to a leader's need for loving people is to know and experience God's love. "God is love" says 1 John 4:8. Love comes from Him. His love is very special and transcends all other kinds of love. It's different from sentimentalism and emotionalism. God's love is around when the other kinds of love run out of gas! It stays with a person in time of crisis and trouble. It's long-lasting and deeply satisfying.

The ancient Greeks knew about different kinds of love. They used at least four different words to describe love. One word expressed physical affection *(eros)*. In a bad sense it referred to sexual immorality. We all understand that "making love" is not always motivated by God's love!

Another word the Greeks used *(storge)* referred to family love, the love of parents for children. It was used of the love among animals. They had another word *(phile)* to express close friendship and companionship. Jesus called His disciples "friends" in John 15:14,15 and the word is *philos*, friendship love.

The most important word for believers is the word *agape*, divine love. When the Bible speaks about God's love that we all need for one another, most of the time it uses *agape*. It's the love that sent Jesus Christ to the cross to die for our sins. The word refers to acts that are unselfish. It is a giving love. It is a concern for the well-being of another person without thought of personal gain. Self-sacrifice is a fundamental idea in the word *agape*. It is a love that does not demand conditions before it is exercised. It is forgiving. It builds up rather than tears down. It always encourages and seeks the best for its object.

The Tragedies of Leadership Without God's Love

First Corinthians 13:1-3 reveals five areas in which God's love is essential or the results are ineffective in the lives of others. Roots as to why leaders fail to motivate others could be found in these verses.

Speech. Leaders must talk. Hopefully, others will listen. If they don't, maybe the problem is that of 1 Corinthians 13:1. Linguistic ability and eloquence may be there, but God's love may be lacking.

I sat down in a plush office one day to talk with a leader about a particular area of disagreement. I was amazed at his eloquence, his command of the English language. The longer he talked, the more uncomfortable I became. I had the feeling he really didn't care about my viewpoint or me personally. The feeling hurt, and I found myself failing to respond to what he was saying. I thought about how often that problem occurs when we talk with people. Sometimes that's all it is, just talk! No love. Just talk. It usually hurts.

Knowledge. Leaders must know things. You can't lead out of ignorance. First Corinthians 13:2 suggests the problem of having great knowledge and understanding, but having no love. Knowledge and love—a difficult balance! The passage says we are nothing if we don't have love, even though we have great knowledge. First Corinthians 8:1 tells us, "Knowledge makes arrogant, but love edifies." It isn't better to be ignorant! That isn't the point! The point is that we need love with knowledge in order to be effective in the lives of others.

One staff member shared with me some time ago about one of her superiors that "he knows what he is talking about; he just doesn't care!" A common problem. Love is essential for knowledge to be helpful.

Faith. Leaders can't operate without faith! But, without love, they are nothing (see 1 Cor. 13:2b)! Removing mountains with faith is a tremendous gift! It's exciting to be around people with great faith. Leaders with faith believe God can do things that most of us have never seen or experienced. Great mountains that seem like insurmountable obstacles to the Lord's work, come tumbling down before the faith of some leaders. Praise the Lord for faith like that! But, without love, the results are minimal in terms of affecting other people.

One pastor with whom I am acquainted challenged his people to great faith. He believed God could do what seemed to be impossible in a particular situation. The trouble is, he was way out in front of the people. He lost them in his zeal. He ran over them in his effort to see God do big things. The people were not with him, and the effort was a colossal failure. What went wrong? The people felt he did not love them. They felt he just wanted to use them to build a great monument to his faith! Faith without love is a tragedy in leadership.

Charity. Leaders should have giving hearts. They should share with people in time of need. First Corinthians 13:3a says, "If I give all my possessions to feed the poor . . . " That's quite a statement! That's charity! Personal sacrifice is involved—"*all my* possessions." It's a great need—"feed the poor." But, without love, there is no profit. The act is not accomplishing what was intended. Charity without love does not do it. All the gifts in the world fail to minister to people when there is no love.

Martyrdom. First Corinthians 13:3b says that even if you gave your body to be burned but didn't have love, it would be a waste of time. Martyrdom for martyrdom's sake is not love. There are many occasions when we play the role of "martyr." This is no guarantee that we love people. It may be just a form of selfishness. People become a martyr in a particular situation in order to receive attention, appreciation, or recognition for what they have done. They want to be noticed.

All of these areas (speech, knowledge, faith, charity, and martyrdom) are important but without love they are not effective in the lives of others. Love enriches those things to the point of building up other people. Selfish motives turn to concern for others when love is controlling these areas. Tragedies in leadership can be changed to triumphs when God's love is operating.

What Does It Mean to Be Concerned for Others?

Leaders must show concern to others. You can't force it; it must come from the heart. But, how do you show concern like that? First Corinthians 13:4 reveals two qualities of God's love that reflect a concern for others rather than yourself.

Patience. What a simple statement—"Love is patient!" Leaders must be patient. Then people know that we really are concerned for them. The Greek word refers to taking a long time to boil. It's always used in reference to people, not things. God is never said to be patient toward things. He doesn't need that kind of patience. He is controlling all things! God does have patience toward people, however. Ephesians 4:2 reminds us that patience toward people involves showing forbearance (literally, putting up with one another) to one another in love. Some people are difficult to work with (in case you hadn't noticed) and to understand. There are times when we must "put up" with them in love. God puts up with us—praise the Lord!

I was very impatient with one of our staff members. His speed and my speed were two different speeds! I wanted him to complete this task on my time schedule! I had a right to expect it from him, I was his boss! He did not finish it on time. He asked for more time. My impatience grew until I was sick of myself! Where was God's love? Absent! Instead of helping him, I was critical and impatient. Lord, forgive me! The situation proved my lack of love. I asked God to forgive me, and tried another way. The other way demonstrated patience. He thanked me for loving him. Will I ever learn?

The ability of leaders to motivate and challenge people will greatly deteriorate if the leader becomes impatient with the people. God's love is patient toward people

Kindness. I like the sound of this word—"kind." The Greek word is used of wine that is mellowed by age. Christ used the word when He said, "My yoke is *easy*" (Matt. 11:30). Submission to Him is not a heavy burden. The experienced ox carries the load. The inexperienced ox (believer) is trained to plow by being loosely tied to the yoke and simply learning from the experienced ox (Christ) alongside him.

Love is like that, it is easy on people, not harsh. It is willing to go alongside people and help them to learn and grow. Galatians 5:22 makes it a part of the "fruit of the Spirit." Ephesians 4:32 uses it with the idea of forgiving one another.

The root idea in the Greek word is that of usefulness.

It's the opposite of harshness or bitterness. Leaders who understand kindness never seek to burden people down. They are easy to get along with and loving in their attitudes. They seek to help, not hurt.

Attitudes That Do Not Belong in a Leader's Life

If God's love is operating in the leader's life, there are certain attitudes that will not be evident. That's the point of 1 Corinthians 13:4b-6 where eight negatives are listed. Here are eight things that love will not do.

Love is not jealous. This word is often used in a good sense and translated "zeal." It is important to be zealous in areas that are good and productive. But, it can lead to jealousy. The desire to have the same things for yourself that another person has is jealousy. Leaders are guilty at times of comparing themselves with other leaders. They start wanting what someone else has. When it becomes a constant habit and begins to control you, you become intensely jealous. God's love is no longer working in your heart.

How do you handle the successes of others when they are brought to your attention? Learn to rejoice! God holds you responsible for what you have done and for what you can do, not for what someone else has done. Thank the Lord for His blessings on others and for the ministry they have. Don't start desiring it! After all, experience tells us that they've got problems you don't need or want!

Love does not brag. Clement of Alexandria (early church leader) says bragging is ornamenting oneself with emphasis on the extraneous and useless! God's love has something to brag about, but not about that which is useless or self-centered.

God's love does not boast about achievements which God's grace has made possible, unless that boasting

177

gives all the glory and credit to God Himself. It is quite easy to brag about things that do not really count in terms of human relationships or eternal values. God's love is different, and people notice!

The pastor who preceded me in my present ministry (also my spiritual father) was showing me the new buildings that our church was constructing. I was considering the pastorate of the church at that time, but found myself a little hesitant about the awesome responsibilities and the possible debt that was being incurred by the congregation. Not knowing what to say, I said to him, "This is a tremendous undertaking. It must make you very proud to think this congregation could build such a large plant." He responded by saying, "David, remember, the church is not the buildings. If the Lord comes tonight, the Antichrist is going to have a big debt!" I don't remember whether that was encouraging to me at that time, but it sure put things in a proper perspective! I gave him the opportunity to brag a little, and he avoided it. Instead, I received an important lesson.

The buildings are not important. God's people are! Boasting in that which is extraneous or useless is a violation of God's love. It shows that our focus is wrong—it's on things, instead of people.

Love is not arrogant. The Greek word means "to blow" and it's used in the middle voice meaning "to blow itself up." God's love does not parade in front of others, constantly inflating one's importance, abilities, or achievements. Proverbs 27:2 says, "Let another praise you, and not your own mouth." A sure sign of the lack of love is arrogance. That which "puffs up" or "blows itself up" is knowledge (1 Cor. 8:1). Leaders can fall into this trap quite easily because of their knowledge of things that others around them do not have.

Love does not act unbecomingly. To put it another

way, God's love is not without shape. Our word "tact" would fit here. Etiquette is involved. God's love is not rude. It says the proper things at the proper time in the loving way.

Many of us mean well, but we are not concerned with how it affects others and so we reveal that God's love is not controlling the way in which we say things to people. What you say may be good and right, but the manner in which you say it can greatly affect the way in which the people respond to you. Love is tactful.

Love does not seek its own. Selfishness is not God's love. Wanting things your way is not love. God's love is filled with humility. It regards others as more important than yourself (see Phil. 2:3,4). What concerns others must be important to the spiritual leader.

The staff meeting we had one day was pursuing ideas for a particular ministry. Everyone was sharing what he or she felt was the best idea. It was good to a point. All of a sudden, we all felt a little selfish. We realized we were not concerned with how our ideas were affecting others. It's amazing how quickly a time like that can change when another's viewpoint is considered! The ideas were then qualified and controlled. It became loving, rather than selfish. Wanting things our way comes naturally. We don't really have to work on it!

Love is not provoked. The word "provoke" is based on the Greek word "'to sharpen." Love is not made sharp by others. It does not get bitter by the reactions and criticisms of others.

Paul was provoked once. He was reacting (see Acts 17:16) to the idolatry of Athens. He wasn't provoked at people, but at idolatry. There is a world of difference! There are times when we ought to get upset and stirred about things and situations that are wrong and which clearly violate God's Word. But, God's love does not get upset with people. Spiritual leaders must learn the difference.

Love does not take into account a wrong suffered. These are the words of an accountant. The idea is that of calculating. God's love is forgiving, not holding a grudge against someone who has offended you. We are calculating when we let our minds dwell on the wrong that people have done to us. It's a form of self-centeredness. It is necessary to bury things that people do to us and to stop dwelling on them.

A friend shared with me one day that the reason he did what he did to a certain person was to get back at him for something that happened many years ago. How tragic! He carried a root of bitterness for many years. He calculated concerning the wrong done to him. He could not forgive, let alone forget.

Love does not rejoice in unrighteousness, but rejoices with the truth. At the sight or sound of evil in others, how do you react? God's love refrains from rejoicing, but rather is saddened. This phrase deals with a censorious spirit, one that condemns others for the sins in their lives.

It's easy to be glad at another's misfortune, especially when it might lead to your gain or will put you in a better light before others. But this is not the way of God's love. God's love has no need of tearing others down in order to feel important. It doesn't rejoice at the failures of others.

One day our staff was discussing the problems of a church nearby. It was declining. We were taking comfort in the fact that our church was growing. It seemed like we were happy to hear of the other church's problems. I felt sick inside. It was wrong, and I knew it. To help my own attitude, I put the other church's ministry on my prayer list and called the pastor one day to encourage him. My attitude changed. I really wanted him to succeed. The experience meant a great deal to me. In a small way, I felt love for him and his ministry. I've asked the Lord to help me to be sympathetic and compassionate when hearing of another's misfortune. Some day I may have a problem and I hope others will care.

How Do You React to Changing Circumstances?

God's love can help. Things don't always turn out the way we think or plan. When changes come, love can sustain us and encourage us. First Corinthians 13:7 mentions four things that will characterize our reactions to the "all things" of life when God's love is controlling.

Love bears all things. The Greek word means to protect or preserve by covering. In modern Greek it refers to the roof of a house. The idea here is that God's love puts up a shelter to shield or cover others.

There are many situations and circumstances in which this kind of reaction is needed in the life of the spiritual leader. He protects and covers those who work with him. He is their defender. He sticks up for them, even though he knows there are problems in their lives. His love is willing to bear these things when others would not be so patient. He concentrates on building people, and that takes time!

Love believes all things. This doesn't mean we're gullible or naive. It rather indicates a confidence and trust in everything that is happening. God is behind it all. It all has a purpose. This belief is the opposite of one who is always doubting things as to why they happen or should have happened.

A spiritual leader learns to rely upon God and His Word, not upon his feelings or whether things are going the way he planned. He trusts the sovereignty of God and knows that at times there will be "setbacks." These become stepping-stones when your trust is in the Lord.

The people who work for a spiritual leader who rests in the Lord, even in times of great stress and change, will find themselves coping with situations that might otherwise seem impossible to handle.

Love hopes all things. We must be optimistic. God's love looks to the future. It bases its response upon the character and power of God. God is able to do what to some seems impossible. Love always hopes for the best. It sees the "all things" as opportunities for God to work and demonstrate who He really is.

This kind of love is not easily discouraged. It's always trusting in what can be done, not dwelling on what was in the past or the trouble in the present. People respond readily to a love that hopes. They are encouraged. They will keep going in their work even under the most difficult circumstances.

Love endures all things. Love can take the pressure. The Greek word means "to remain under." It's used of things or situations, not people. Love bears up under difficult circumstances. It knows how to keep going when others drop out. It cares enough to stay when things are not going the way people want.

A pastor informed me that he was quitting his church. He was discouraged. The growth was not there that he wanted. He was impatient. He did not want to be associated with a declining church. I simply asked him, "Do you love those people?" He wasn't sure that was important. It was. God's love will keep you going when most people want to quit. God's love will endure under the most trying circumstances.

What Chance Do We Have of Experiencing God's Love?

God's love is produced in our hearts through the pres-

182

ence and power of the Holy Spirit (see Rom. 5:5; Gal. 5:22). Every believer, because of the indwelling of the Holy Spirit (see 1 Cor. 6:19,20), has the capacity to experience God's love every day of his life. The potential is there. The application may be the problem. Being controlled by the Holy Spirit in order to love as God wants and as you need is the root problem in spiritual leadership. The great need is for Spirit-filled leaders.

Formulas have been suggested before as to how to experience a Spirit-filled life. Conditions such as prayer, faith, obedience, witness, study, etc., have all been proposed as "secrets" to a Spirit-filled life. It seems to fall in the category of what I call the "more syndrome." If I just do something "more" than what I'm doing now, I will achieve the desired result of being Spirit-filled. That can be very discouraging and self-defeating. How much is "more"? Do I need more prayer? Of course, always! Do I need more obedience? Of course, always!

To simplify this problem of being Spirit-filled, I began by recognizing that the Holy Spirit is God. He is fully capable of manifesting God's love in my life. He really doesn't need my help in one sense. I often get in the way of what He wants to do. I don't really need to worry about what He does.

Next, I realized that one thing stops the flow of God's power in my life—sin! It grieves and quenches the Spirit. My simple conclusion: Get rid of the sin and the filling of the Spirit is automatic! You may not like the simplicity of this, but it helps me, and it may help you! If sin stops the ministry of the Spirit, then that's the problem I need to deal with. Let's try an example for better understanding.

I had a problem showing love to a particular person. Everything I tried failed. Things got worse. One day I realized the problem, I had an unforgiving spirit toward something that person had done. Once that sin was removed, my love toward the person was restored. Very simple.

Another example: I deeply offended another staff member by an action I took as a spiritual leader. I felt at that time that I should apologize but I simply neglected to do so. Much later I discovered a serious problem in loving that staff member. Finally, after much internal struggle, I went to that person and apologized for what I had done many months before. The relationship was restored and love was now expressed freely between us.

The examples are numerous. Sin is blocking the flow of God's love. Deal with sin, and you'll experience God's love again. Above all, don't put things off that you know you should do (like seeking forgiveness). Deal with things immediately. The love pattern will be more consistent.

Leader's Checklist

1. What attitudes do you have that do not belong in a leader's life?
2. Are you weak in any of the five areas in which God's love is essential? Which one(s)? What can you do to strengthen them?
3. How do you demonstrate patience and kindness?
4. Which of the eight negatives do you need to work on in your own life?
5. Is your love optimistic, looking to the future?
6. How do you react to changing circumstances?
7. How can you experience God's love in your life?

THE BOTTOM LINE: ARE YOU A LEADER?

Leaders are made, not born! That's the point behind this whole book. We named seven essentials that reveal what a spiritual leader is really like: example, communication, ability, motivation, authority, strategy, and love. But, how does a person know for sure that he or she is a spiritual leader, especially if you've had no experience at leadership? Where do you start?

Leadership Is Not for Everyone!

Some people believe that every person can be and should be a leader. If every person was a leader, who would do the following? No, leadership isn't for everyone. Experience shows that very clearly. Some people try to be leaders only to discover that no one is following them. Others cannot take the pressure and demands of leadership. Some cannot make decisions or give direction to others. Some don't like the loneliness and isolation. Leadership really isn't for everyone!

There are degrees of leadership. Some do well with a group of 10 people but fail in leading 1,000 people. There are enormous differences in the leadership of 10 when compared with 1,000. The demands and responsibilities vary greatly.

There are different styles of leadership. Some like to work at desks, and some like motivating people to action. Some handle the training of the few, and others do well with motivating crowds. Some are rigid and inflexible; others are easy-going and constantly changing.

So, what is a leader, and how do you know that you are one? What is necessary to prove your leadership if you would like to be a leader but have no experience at it?

Leadership Evaluation

There are certain things by which leadership can be evaluated or tested. One of these tests is not enough to prove you are a leader. All of them help to confirm whether you are a leader or not.

Test 1—the call of God. In spiritual leadership, it is imperative that a person knows God has called him to a role of leadership. But how does God do that? Do you open the Bible and the first verse you see is the one that God will use to speak to you? Do you hear voices in the night? Does it come through a dream? Do you hear bells ringing? Does lightning flash from the sky? Of course not. Then how do you know if God has called you to spiritual leadership?

The call of God is a continual impression on your heart that makes you desire to be a spiritual leader. If you really don't want to be a spiritual leader, then don't get involved. Concerning leaders for the local church, Paul wrote to Timothy (see 1 Tim. 3:1) that men should desire the office of leadership. The Greek text emphasizes an intense desire that a man feels in and of himself, not something that someone else has pressured him into doing. If God is calling you, the desire should be strong and constant. If it comes and goes, or if you can take it or leave it, then leave it. Don't get involved!

Test 2—personal desire. This flows out of the call of God. Do you want to be a leader? Do you really? Leaders who lack a strong personal desire for leadership are usually ineffective and weak leaders. You must really want it and enjoy it. Too many leaders complain about the responsibilities of leadership.

One of the men in our church was constantly complaining about his responsibilities as a leader. Everyone else was the problem, and his work load was too great to bear. He made it difficult for people to work with him. He was unbearable at times. He had a critical spirit. He liked the spiritual limelight that being a leader brought to him. He wanted to be noticed. Today he does not have a position of leadership. You might say he lost it. I would say it is doubtful that he ever had it. All the time he was in a position of leadership, he lacked the personal desire and joy of being a leader. One who has the desire enjoys the responsibilities of leadership and gladly assumes them.

Test 3—maturity. Forget about spiritual leadership if you are still a baby Christian or you have not been growing in your knowledge of Christ. Maturity is essential for spiritual leadership. Maturity is necessary in order to discern whether or not you are a spiritual leader.

Just because you have had leadership in the secular world, do not conclude that spiritual leadership will come easy for you. Without maturity in Christ, you will fall flat on your face! You'll run into problems you never thought existed! You'll be hurt and often discouraged, and you'll probably give up in utter frustration!

Test 4—experience. The old saying, "You'll never know until you try," would apply here. It's tough to know if you are a leader when you have never led any-

187

one! Experience is vital to bringing you confidence and assurance of your spiritual leadership. Don't go through your Christian life wondering if you should or could have been a leader! Start experiencing it!

Start small. Don't go up to your pastor and say, "I would like to be the leader for that class of 200 people!" If he's smart, he won't give that kind of responsibility to someone without any experience as a spiritual leader. Take on a little responsibility within the framework of somebody else's leadership. Be faithful in a few things, and your leadership will grow to many things.

One of the strong leaders in our ministry today started by following up a new convert. Later, after proving his faithfulness in that responsibility, he took a small Bible class (discipleship group) of three men, and worked with them. Before too long, he taught a Sunday School class and proved his leadership ability. He started extending his ministry into other areas, slowly and faithfully. He was dependable. He developed a ministry on his own. He then became part-time staff and eventually a full-time pastor. When he started, we all wondered about his ability to be a leader. Time and experience proved he was.

The most important thing to remember in gaining experience for spiritual leadership is to be faithful and dependable. It may be a small and insignificant ministry to you, but do it with all your heart! Those who are faithful in the small things, have a way of being used in larger areas of ministry. Those who are not dependable, in spite of having many opportunities, never become strong spiritual leaders.

Test 5—confirmation by others. Does anyone else think you are a leader (besides your father and mother)! Before you judge whether you are a spiritual leader or not, you'd better consider what others are saying. That's why time is necessary in evaluating spiritual leaders. It takes time to observe people in action. It takes time to determine faithfulness and dependability.

A few years ago, one of the young men in our church felt that God wanted him to be a spiritual leader. He communicated that to us as he should have done. One thing was missing: confirmation by others. When people were asked concerning his effectiveness, much doubt and question about him were expressed. We waited a little longer (good advice!). The people in the area of ministry where he was working were not convinced of his leadership. Maybe they were wrong. Perhaps it was something personal. Let's give him the benefit of a doubt. We checked with others in another area of ministry. Same report. Much doubt as to whether he was a leader was continually reflected in these discussions. Our only choice? We decided not to use him in a particular leadership role until his spiritual leadership became more evident to those with whom he worked.

The counsel of other members of the Body of Christ is vital to the determination of spiritual leadership. If everyone questions the person's leadership, it is doubtful that any effective leadership can be exercised!

Test 6—results. Are there any results occurring from the exercise of your leadership? Were goals reached? Were people challenged, discipled, and enlisted? Was the response of the people positive?

Goals that are specific and measurable are vital to determining the results of spiritual leadership. Goals form a solid basis for evaluation.

One summer I saw a man's leadership exercised in a most revealing way as he mobilized, on his own, over 500 people to do some maintenance work on our church facilities. Some may have questioned his leadership but the results proved he was a leader! He accomplished the goals he set out to complete within the time period designated and the funds allowed.

Results can be seen in the lives of people whom the spiritual leader has trained and motivated. Are they productive people? That speaks well for the leadership of the one who poured his time and energy into them. It isn't always noticed by outsiders, but real leadership can be evaluated by how effective the people are who work for him or under him.

Other results to be evaluated are efficiency and happiness among those working with the leader. When things are in constant turmoil, there is a question about the leadership.

Test 7—knowledge. What do you know about leadership? Have you read books on it? They will help. None of them are the final answer to being a leader, but they won't hurt you! Have you attended any leadership seminars or conferences? What principles of leadership and management do you know?

It is my personal conviction that seminaries and graduate schools preparing people for spiritual leadership should have courses in their curriculum which deal with spiritual leadership. These courses should not only require reading in the fields of leadership and management, but should also seek ways to give students valuable experience in exercising leadership.

Learn all you can about leadership. There are many books available (both sacred and secular). Learn also from the lives of those who are spiritual leaders. Study what they do and how they do it. Learn from the many biblical examples of spiritual leaders. Knowledge of leadership will aid you in the development of your own leadership.

Take these seven tests and evaluate yourself. Is the evidence of each test strong, meaning a continual thing with you? Or is it weak, meaning that the test can only be applied in a few situations? The category of "weak" would indicate the necessity of more time and opportunity for evaluation. Maybe the evidence is not there yet in your life. If so, mark the category "none."

Tests of Leadership	None	Weak	Strong
1. The call of God			
2. Personal desire			
3. Maturity			
4. Experience			
5. Confirmation by others			
6. Results			
7. Knowledge			

Don't be discouraged by past experience or present difficulties. The Lord can make you the leader He wants you to be! Trust Him, and rely upon His power and strength! If leadership is your desire, pray every day that God would develop and strengthen your leadership. Ask Him to give you wisdom for that leadership.

Sometimes you will feel that being a leader is not worth it. You will receive complaints and criticisms from people because you are in the position of leadership. Everything won't turn out the way you expected or planned. There will be conflicts and personality problems. People will get upset and hurt over the way you handle things. Others will oppose you and resist your leadership. It will be easy at times to say "I quit." Remove those words from your vocabulary right now! Never quit! You may change things or situations but don't ever quit!

One day it will be worth it all to hear our Saviour say, "Well done, good and faithful servant." It is His approval that we want! It's worth it, my leader friend, not only for future reward but for present blessings. Leadership is not easy but it's worth it! I love it, do you? I wouldn't want things different in my life in terms of leadership. I want to be a leader. I don't deserve to be, but I want it! I want to do the best job I possibly can for the glory of my Lord Jesus Christ! I need His help every day, and that's obvious to all who work with me! I'm not perfect, and I don't know all there is to know about leadership. But, I'm trying. I'm working at it, and so should you! We all can learn. Every person and every situation is our teacher!

Leaders are made, not born! Therefore, there's hope for all of us! The Lord can make us into the leaders He wants us to be! Praise His wonderful name!